Dearest ArKan,

Here it is my First Book!
Complete with my crazy little
Stories

Here's to new adventures
those that Brave heart

RUNWAY
and set the
soul A sail.
BIRD

lot of love

This book is dedicated to the love of my life,
MJ River, and to my Mum and Dad

IRINA LAZAREANU

RUNWAY BIRD

A ROCK 'N' ROLL
STYLE GUIDE

Flammarion

Fragments from my journals offer a glimpse into my childhood in the Old World. Long before these thoughts and inspirations became words in the crucible of this book, they had to break through the Iron Curtain.

Page 6: Portrait by Jan Welters.

Contents

Foreword

There are dazzling beauties in fashion. Irina is one of them. Some pass through, vanishing with rapture into the world of fashion images and in the spirit of the times, disappearing with the designs that they had so luminously incarnated. And then there are the unforgettable models like Irina: women whose grace, attitudes, and looks do not easily disappear, even from a world saturated with fashion imagery.

Why does the vision of Irina persist? It goes beyond nostalgia for the decade from 2000–10 — the last years before the digital age and the dominance of the virtual world today. It goes beyond the Romanian and somber beauty of a mysterious time that she inspires — that of a warring and violent Europe, which we will remember for generations.

There are no rules, only exceptions.

What makes Irina exceptional? Her fragility as a dark angel who captures the zeitgeist, the music of the moment, and the crazy generosity of the early 2000s that wasn't yet fully digitalized, at that watershed point of no return in the history of the world. She knew how — with innocence, truth, and simplicity — to give shape to her life. To invent through fashion and music, and through the people she encountered, a *form to life and to survival* that was as photographic as it was artistic, friendly and social, and which amplified current fashions, the depth of her beauty and the durability of her image.

This book bears witness to the final years when being present still required presence: the pulse of sensitivity, attitude and a true singularity that was not recomposed, virtualized or digitized.

Olivier Zahm

Portrait by Inez &
Vinoodh before
a *V* magazine shoot
for the fall 2007
issue no. 48.

Introduction

Becoming Irina

Hi. I'm Rini. Pleased to meet you.

Before we walk down the rock 'n' roll catwalk together, let me introduce myself. If we go right back to the start, I was never supposed to find a meaningful career in fashion ... or even to live in this part of the world. I was born in Romania in 1982, under the rule of a brutal dictator. It was a dark time when the government controlled everything and everyone, a period in the country's history when the population was starving and people would disappear without a trace. The Iron Curtain that contained us was a barrier to the freedom of expression, and it cut my family off from the rest of the world.

My childhood was tough, worlds apart from what we might consider a conventional environment. By the time I was five years old I found myself in a refugee camp, which forced me to grow up real fast, exposing me to certain truths and life lessons that I carry with me to this day. I learned to be patient, to be invisible, to survive.

Yet everything comes to pass. Nothing comes to stay.

Somehow I ended up in Canada and later in Europe, and serendipitously became that girl: in the right place at the right time, where the planets aligned and destiny took its course.

There was always a part of me that felt like I didn't belong in fashion, like I didn't deserve all those blessings that were bestowed upon my soul. Maybe there's a part of me that still feels like I cheated the odds in a simple twist of fate.

What else can I tell you about myself? I've always been a traveller, a feral daughter of the road. I'm a hyperactive, wild-eyed child of the sun. Curious to a fault, I'm a sponge for random facts and useless information. I love reading people; I notice when they listen and watch when they speak.

What do you need to know about this book? Style is a poem that expresses the zeitgeist. Fashion has remained a constant cultural voice throughout the years. Historically, what you wear and how you wear it have always been powerful tools of self-expression for rebels and free thinkers: a fluid uniform, a movable feast.

At its core, this book is a love letter to the magical people I've been blessed to meet throughout my twenty years in fashion. Of the countless folk I've encountered, the ones you'll find lurking here are those whose influence impacted me the most, those whose spell endures. Some challenged me, some taught me how to dress, others taught me how to love. In this book I'll share what I've learned from them about style and attitude. And while beauty may seduce you on the road to truth, getting through the voyage in style certainly never hurts.

I've made a case study of each of my subjects to decode rock 'n' roll's long love affair with fashion. We'll break down why their various looks work so well, and give you tips on how you can recreate them by weaving them into your own individual style.

This is gonna be fun. Let's get started, shall we?

Portrait by Jan Welters for French *Elle,* May 2008.

Page 12: From a Pierre Cardin shoot by Thierry Le Gouès.

Under the Influence

FASHION

Backstage with Agyness Deyn at John Galliano F/W 2007–8 RTW.

RUNWAY BIRDS

and Supermodels

To be nobody-but-yourself - in a world
which is doing its best, night and day,
to make you everybody else - means to fight
the hardest battle which any human being can fight.

E. E. Cummings

They were strong,
confident women,
who fascinated us all
with their undeniable
wit and enduring charm.

THE BACKSTAGE OF A CATWALK SHOW
is a beautiful and chaotic organism. Fashion week is a
travelling circus, an elaborate production with a mood,
character and energy that change from city to city and
according to each designer. The 'variable constants' in this
equation are the show girls – the runway birds who, while simultaneously
retaining the unique and individual aesthetic for which they were
recruited, are versatile enough to project each designer's vision.

Shows are emotionally and physically draining. You become a
veteran in the field of sleep deprivation and an expert on partying while
developing an alarmingly high tolerance for alcohol consumption.

Oh, and lest I forget, amidst all this, you're expected to walk at the
same time. Sound easy? Like that time photographer David Sims asked
me to 'jump and not move'.

There are as many rules for surviving a season on the catwalk as there
are stars in the sky, but I would suggest, in a manner of speaking, that it's
no use sitting around waiting for a good hand of cards; fortune favours the
brave and you have to make your own luck. It can be an unpredictable
flight of frenzy, so make sure you sit by the emergency exit.

In the 1990s, models suddenly became larger than life in the collective
consciousness. Sure, previous top models bewitched us, but the
mythology of the supermodel – curated in large part by Gianni Versace
and Azzedine Alaïa – began with the Magnificent Seven, amidst rumours
of 'We don't wake up for less than $10,000 a day'.

Yes, they were dreamy, otherworldly creatures, enchanting and
charismatic. They exuded confidence, a killer sense of style and endless
panache. They became pillars of the fashion industry – each with a
singular style that was equally modern and timeless. Their iconic and
quintessential beauty exerted influence over generations. The huge
eyes, the perfect cheekbones, the ridiculously long legs (seriously, you
need a ladder to climb up those things) were surpassed only by the
hilariously dry sense of humour these women shared.

But in my experience, they were first and foremost strong, confident
women, who fascinated us all with their undeniable wit and enduring
charm. Today, these achingly talented Renaissance women are all career
multi-hyphenates and multitaskers with the ability to reinvent themselves
as entrepreneurs, philanthropists, activists, mothers, muses.

When my fellow runway birds and I were taking our first catwalk steps, the girls from previous years – Carmen Kass, Angela Lindvall, Shalom Harlow, Carolyn Murphy, Mariacarla Boscono – took us under their wings and showed us the ropes. There were about twenty-five girls who worked every major show across the globe, most of us doing upwards of sixty shows a season. I began clocking up seventy to ninety shows and, in 2007, I broke a record for the most shows ever walked by a model in a single season. I also kinda broke myself in the process, though: mind, body and soul.

My schedule consisted of walking three to five shows a day and getting several fittings for shows to be held the following day. Most fittings took place at night, sometimes wrapping up at 5 am, when I would go home to shower before heading back out to my first show by 7 am. You don't have to be a maths wizard to figure out that there's not much time left for sleep.

On my few evenings off, I felt obliged to show my face at industry parties, regularly running myself into the ground before the close of the first fashion week in NYC. Adrenaline spiked and the only way I was able to avoid collapsing was to just keep going, sleeping only when my body would crash, which happened from time to time. I relied heavily on my team of agents, managers and drivers (badasses in superhero capes) to somehow keep me on point.

On the catwalk
for Anna Molinari
F/W 2007–8
RTW in Milan.

Cheri Bowen was my agent in New York – she's a captain booker, North Star and full-time ball buster. She had the unfortunate task of managing my work diary and the even less fortunate job of keeping track of me. Her eye still twitches when she recalls my tendency during that time to 'disappear faster than Houdini' whenever she'd blink.

I would systematically bribe her with Balenciaga bags and Chanel jewellery during shows, just so she would let me stay up one hour past my bedtime (a very effective technique). *Sleepless in Manhattan* sums up my first ten years in the Big Apple, and 2007 was no exception. Looking back now, I can see how irrational my decisions were, but in those days, as far as I was concerned, all I needed in the morning was a cup of joe, cigarettes and some good tunes in my headphones.

London and Milan followed the same rigorous and exhausting schedule, so by the time I got to Paris – my sometime home and stomping ground – I was running on fumes. So I brought in my very own secret weapon: Miss Sally Anchassi. Sally was both my best friend and an agent extraordinaire. She kept me afloat in the face of impossible odds, organising my schedule, my meetings, my interviews and fittings and making sure I didn't die! She somehow always got us from point A to point B right on time.

Her previous work experience included managing the Babyshambles music tour; I believe the Vatican is considering her for sainthood. She's funny, charismatic and rules with an iron fist. Don't be fooled by her sweet demeanour or petite stature; I've seen her make grown men cry and she can win an argument with a mere glance. Not surprising, then, that Bruce Willis fell in love with her after only a casual dinner encounter. But she didn't have time for Bruce; he was interfering with her schedule. 'Damn it, people, we're late for Dior!' she said, leaving a broken-hearted Bruce on a Parisian street corner as she chirruped at the driver to 'giddy up and go'.

With Freja Beha
in Prague,
July 2006, for
W magazine by
Michael Thompson.

Ultimately, the runway birds got me through it all – the pressure, the sleep deprivation – and when we were together, it was easy to be nobody-but-myself.

During fashion weeks, the eyes of the world were fixed upon us. Every word and every move down to our micro facial expressions were dissected and examined by photographers, the critics, the press. The more experienced models gave invaluable advice when it felt like things were moving too fast and the ground was shifting under my feet. Once I became a seasoned veteran, I found myself carrying on the tradition of looking after the new girls. I packed plasters, Benadryl and chocolate, and kept an eye out for everything from impending meltdowns to lingering creeps. Some girls would break into hives backstage, while others wound up with bloody and blistered feet. The chocolate? That was for the youngest ones, who often arrived unprepared and pretty much alone. Wide-eyed, vulnerable kids whose genetic quirks – considered the right kind of beautiful du jour – had fast-tracked them into the murky world of fashion.

My home in Paris was a kind of base camp sanctuary for misfits and kindred spirits alike, and I'd throw secret fashion week parties just for us runway birds. Sweet Lily Cole stayed with me for a while, and Freja Beha and I were attached at the hip. My wonderful friend Tasha Tilberg lived down the road, Lily Donaldson sometimes graced us with her presence and Agyness Deyn got tangled up in our web of awesomeness. One thing I've learned about myself throughout the years is that I sure know how to throw a party (I also know how to get thrown *out* of one). Cue the 1980s music, the champagne (or wine from a box), the butterfly wings, the hats, the Chanel necklaces, the capes and the tutu princess dresses. Tiaras to Christmas decorations, it all came out to play. My blinds were closed and my living room floor was our stage. For those few hours we could be silly: freely, simply, us.

Ultimately, the runway birds got me through it all – the pressure, the sleep deprivation – and when we were together, it was easy to be nobody-but-myself. We formed a bond that would last a lifetime, making memories from the silly details, the laughter that got us through trials and tribulations, the random acts of kindness. Those moments are etched in my memory; they are the ones that define me.

With Jessica Stam
and Lily Donaldson
backstage at Fendi,
F/W 2007–8
RTW in Milan.

DIOR SIXTIETH ANNIVERSARY

Paris fashion week is undeniably the crown jewel event within the industry. The most extravagant shows delivered by the world's most iconic and renowned designers — lavish sets, glamorous outfits, in short, creatively expansive yet wildly decadent productions with XXL budgets.

Some of my most unforgettable runway experiences took place in the city of light, most notably the Dior sixtieth anniversary at Versailles. Dear Prudence, what a day! Let's face it, brilliance gushes from John Galliano.

Along the halls of The Orangery was the longest catwalk I've ever walked — nearly a mile! To be honest, though, it felt more like ten in those heels. The show's casting was a Who's Who of supermodels: Linda, Naomi, Amber, Shalom, Gisele — the list went on.

That season, John transformed his muses into three-dimensional interpretations of works by impressionist and modern painters. Every model was given a brief for a pseudo-theatrical role to help her get into character. Gisele became the Black Wasp, Helena Christensen was Catherine the Great. I became Kiki de Montparnasse in an outfit he had designed with my 'playful personality' in mind.

The energy backstage was frenetic! We all felt this show might be remembered as an important moment in the history of fashion. The excitement was palpable. As it turns out, gathering sixty supermodels in one regal environment makes for a captivating storyline.

Without giving too much away, I'm sure you can imagine the narrative twists and turns such a rogue's gallery of characters could create. There was enough diva drama around to make Marie Antoinette blush.

For starters, a certain supermodel was missing in action. Her private jet was sitting on a runway fuelled and ready to go. She, however, was experiencing some technical difficulties with her significant other due to unpredictable weather patterns caused by his insufferable attitude.

There were three separate makeup tents assigned to different ranks: 'model', 'supermodel', or 'super supermodel'. Whoever had this brilliant idea wasn't long for this world. Ranking supermodels in order of importance isn't something any mortal should ever attempt.

After five hours of hair and makeup and several bottles of champagne, Kiki was coming to life. I was covered in glitter and feathers and was methodically getting into character. Laughing and giggling myself towards the runway, I quickly realised that no one could actually walk in the shoes. 'Screw it', shouted Naomi, 'we'll float down the runway.' A mere fender bender for this group of all-stars, who, of course, pulled it off gracefully. A magical show, exquisite and delightful, it was perfect and — like all of John's shows — we had fun, maybe a little *too* much fun at the lavish after-party, considering half of us barely made it to Chanel the next morning.

Backstage at the Dior sixtieth anniversary F/W 2007–8 Couture show in Versailles in July 2007.

CHILDREN AND DOVES

VERSACE
AND PRINCE

So let me set the scene: It's September 2006 at Versace's Spring 2007 collection, Palazzo Versace, via Gesù in Milan. The sexiest show on the planet. Donatella had invited Prince to perform at her after-party. Girls, boys, we were all beyond excited at the prospect of snatching a glance of The Myth, The Legend, The Sexiest Showman on Earth.

We were lining up backstage for first looks when I became aware of a collective shiver surging through the ranks.

There. He. Was.

His Purple Highness. Manifesting himself like a magical leprechaun in a dapper regal outfit complete with cane, he moved ethereally past the girls. I even think one particularly scrawny Italian chick nearly fainted. Or wait, was that me?

Anyway, just before he turned a corner and disappeared into infamy, Lily Donaldson mustered up enough courage and spoke for us all as she managed a hoarse: 'We love you, Prince!' What happened next made our knees buckle. Gliding to a majestic halt, the sexy MF turned his head and replied: 'I love you too, baby.'

Yep. Swoon.

I was trying to recover from this surreal moment when the show started. Members of the production team were running around, the hair and makeup teams were doing their last-minute retouches, and our lovely seamstresses were methodically checking our dresses for minor adjustments when they suddenly realised my mini corset dress was too loose 'à la poitrine' (my breasts are like two fried eggs on the wall, a fact that had never been a problem for previous runway shows).

But this was Versace! Where sexy figures are accentuated and celebrated, where boobies are a thing! The gravitas of the situation set in. I wasn't going to fill in those cups without surgical intervention and time was running out.

So a seamstress hastily threw two silicon chicken cutlets down my bustier, said a prayer, and wished me luck!

Doing my best to keep a straight face, I stepped up to the front of the line where Donatella gave me a little slap on the bum and urged me to 'Walk like you've never walked before'.

With the boss's words ringing in my ears, I charged down the runway, stomping like a raging stallion, swinging my hips and silently channelling Beyoncé, when, with a sickly sinking sensation, I felt a cutlet slowly slipping down my dress.

I could imagine the horrific scene — the paradox to glamour — if a pair of chicken cutlets were to slap down in the middle of the Versace podium. I couldn't let this happen; Prince was performing, for Pete's sake! So, in my infinite wisdom, I slowly began bending backwards like a limbo-dancing pretzel. I continued this inexplicable manoeuvre until, by the time I had circled backstage, the whole team was wondering if I might be having a stroke.

The Versace S/S 2007 RTW in Milan. Backstage with Freja (top right), on the catwalk (center) and at the after-party with Angela Lindvall.

Punk Rocker

Agy Deyn has never been one to follow fashion trends (she couldn't be bothered). She instinctively follows her gut to create her look. She's not afraid to take chances or to make mistakes. Punk is chaos, mayhem, disorder. But sometimes from chaos comes beauty. A punk bird is much more than just a pretty face rocking heavy Docs and a distinctively badass style. There's proper substance in Agy's character, an undeniable personality that effortlessly informs her uncontrived street style, a reflection of that authenticity. She is spirited, independent and fearless in her wardrobe choices. Not some kind of fragile chick whose opinion shifts whichever way the wind blows on Wuthering Heights.

We shared a tiny room in Milan during one of our first fashion weeks. I was struck by her infectiously positive spirit. Her audacious sense of humour pretty much kept me sane. The bands Agy turned me on to – The Fall, A Certain Ratio, The Nosebleeds, Alberto y Lost Trios Paranoias, Cairo – they brought me joy through the long hours. And the fact that she showed me how to boil water to make pasta ultimately kept me from starving to death.

Above: Agy in New York.

Facing page: Agy on stage in London.

Dr. Martens

DIY Style

I once wore Dr. Martens with a Chanel couture dress on the red carpet of a major awards show. Everyone was shocked and appalled and told me off, but then Mr Lagerfeld thought it was brilliant so it immediately became a thing: from fashion faux pas to a fashion 'do' within minutes.

1 You can pair Dr. Martens with pretty much anything:
- **short shorts and a T-shirt** in the summer
- **fancy dresses** if you want to make an outfit less pretentious
- **jeans and a leather jacket** if you're going for that iconic rocker look

2 Or you can play around with **brightly coloured laces**! Try four different hues; be bold, be colourful and be loud.

3 Write and draw on them with a Tipp-Ex or Wite-Out to make them your own – put your thoughts out there, one step at a time.

Be original, kids. It's a lot sexier than being trendy. Forget about conforming to norms. Your style is as unique as you are and a reflection of your personality.

PRO TIP

Wear thick wool socks to break
in your new Docs (your feet will
be eternally grateful).
Or **buy vintage Docs:** they look
better, they are a lot more
comfortable and you can buy them
for a song.

Facing page: Dr. Martens
echoing mad footsteps
in the night in Paris.

Above: Mood: break
time attitude with Agy
and Freja captured
by Matt Irwin.

Sleek and Sexy

The compelling and enigmatic phenomenon known to the world as Freja Beha is a hypnotically beguiling force to be reckoned with. Though intriguingly spartan with her words, she's known to swoop in with a brilliantly succinct and astute sound bite no matter how dense the conversational topic. Every pithy statement from those 'kiss me if you dare' lips is always followed by a long intense stare with the kind of gaze that carries more sex appeal then an Anaïs Nin novel.

Freja looks good in pretty much anything (or nothing at all for that matter); the achingly cool and laidback energy she exudes sets her apart from and ahead of the pack. When she's not prowling a catwalk or smouldering on set in front of a camera, her personal clothing choices are a masterclass in how to rock a simple, well-cut blazer or one of her trademark suits. This tendency has rightfully cemented her as the modern heiress to the quintessential pioneers who blazed this elegantly androgynous path before her.

Above: Freja at the Rag & Bone F/W 2009–10 RTW in NYC.

Facing page: Test shot by Michael Thompson for the *W* magazine 'Czech Mate' editorial, Prague, 2006.

FOR IRINA.

PRAGUE '06   [signature]

The Slick Suit

Suit Up

The history of women who dared to wear a suit, challenging the status quo and forcing society to accept gender neutrality forever after, dates back to French actress Sarah Bernhardt, who scandalously began wearing boy's clothing in public in 1870. Suffragettes donned suits during their revolutionary voting rights campaign at the turn of the twentieth century, and these civilly disobedient birds inspired Coco Chanel to boldly design the first truly female suit by 1918.

This uniform symbolically and sartorially represented the women's liberation movement. The battle for equality continues today, so imagine how menacing it must have seemed at the time! Sometimes it feels like we're moving backwards, but wasn't it Ginger Rogers who said that she can do everything Fred Astaire does, but backwards and in heels?!

Speaking of heels and suits, well, they make a pretty good couple! High heels can elongate the beautiful tailored silhouette of a fitted suit and simultaneously give the optical illusion of having legs that go on for days. Just like Freja, I am a suit lover and I've worn them in a myriad of ways to 'suit' any occasion.

• **A three-piece suit** (complete with waistcoat) is a great choice for a casual night out if styled properly with a pair of old beat-up Converse and a skinny tie.

• **A complete Vivienne Westwood horseback riding ensemble** with an elaborate, **dramatic corset** is one of my favourite first date outfits for a more theatrical approach. It's my very own chastity belt: if you can figure out how to take it off, then you deserve a reward!

• **A classic oversized tuxedo jacket transformed into a mini dress,** worn with either heels or flat boots, or styled with anything underneath from a body suit to a rock T-shirt – this unconventional way to wear a suit jacket is both original and sexy, and perfect for painting the town red on your girls' night out.

Facing page: A tribute to Yoko Ono, portrait by Jan Welters for French *Elle*, Paris, 2008.

Above: Three snapshots from Irina L., my first fashion collection, released in Japan in 2010.

Lily

Bohème Chic

I've always kinda been in awe of Lily Cole. She's one of those rare creatures who excels at whatever she turns her hand to – it's no wonder she captivated the industry at a tender age with her fairy-tale Victorian beauty. She can be a paragon of the classic ideal of female beauty, but shine equally brightly when placed in a modern or countercultural setting. I was lucky enough to meet Lily when she was just a teenager; she stayed with me when she travelled to Paris for work. She became like a little sister to me (albeit much wiser than me) and I've seen her grow up and navigate her career with grace and elegance. But what really gets me is just how smart the girl is. She could just as easily have decided to become a particle physicist, but her creative nature led her to the theatre and the arts instead.

　　To illustrate just how much of an innately good soul she is, I could start by listing all the philanthropic and conservational causes she throws her time and energy into, but it's quicker just to say that her integrity and kindness should be an inspiration for us all, let alone the leagues of young women who rightfully see her not only as a role model for style, but also for global compassion.

Lily by Max Snow for *Rika Magazine*, issue no. 52011.

The Chiffon Skirt

One Skirt, Three Looks:

1 The chiffon skirt has always been a girl's best friend; it works with many **different body types** and can be advantageous for **tall women**, gracefully dress a **curvaceous lady** or subtly hide **skinny legs.**

2 If, on the contrary, you want to **show off your pins**, recreate J-Lo's leg moment from the Met Gala red carpet by cutting a simple slit up the front.

3 When you're 'over' the long skirt look, **upcycle it into a mini**; all you need is a pair of scissors.

Revisit the Past

Lily's eclectic style – colourful boho chic, or 1950s-inspired silhouettes – calls for vintage skirts. There's an art to finding the right skirt in the right fit. I always find mine in second-hand shops.

- From 1950s **chequered patterns** to 1960s improbably long **floaty folk prints**, pair them with an oversized wool sweater and boots.
- Spoil yourself by investing in a beautiful **mousseline skirt**; look for Chloé or Giambattista Valli.
- Pair a **three-quarters wool skirt** with a tweed jacket topped with a vintage hat for that sought-after Celine look.

Facing page: Snapshot by Martin Laporte during an *Elle* Canada shoot, 2002.

Above: Wearing vintage with Lily, at a party at Karl Lagerfeld's home in Paris, 2007.

Helena

Electric Lady

Peruvian-Dane Helena Christensen is an art connoisseur, music lover, world traveller and a dreamer at heart. She's an icon, but Helena is the first to downplay her supermodel status: 'It's actually very embarrassing being called a supermodel. You don't want to be considered superhuman for being a model'. A phenomenal mother and a gentle soul, she's also a committed animal and environmental rights activist; you're as likely to find her taking a morning dip in a lake in the Catskills as chairing a business meeting in a Copenhagen boardroom. She's achingly glamorous, absolute murder in a pair of high heels!

One of the 'Magnificent Seven', Helena appeared in Chris Isaak's 'Wicked Game' video, which MTV played to death, cementing her position as the thinking kid's celeb crush. In retrospect, she's the rock star supermodel that the 1990s needed: liberated, creative and multitalented. She was her own remarkable invention – like Lee Miller, who went from model and muse for Man Ray and company to becoming one of the most interesting surrealist photographers in the 1920s. Helena learned the tricks of the trade from the very best 'painters of light' of her generation, from Peter Lindbergh to Helmut Newton, distinguishing herself with her inspiring imagery that has been celebrated in exhibitions from New York to Amsterdam and in magazines everywhere. She once told the *Guardian*: 'One of the reasons I started modelling was because I thought it would be a great way to explore my photography. Working with so many extremely talented photographers in a way means I've been in photography school for twenty years.'

Above and facing page: Helena for *Harper's Bazaar* España, July–August 2020, issue no. 119, styled by Camilla Staerk.

Style Uncovered

No one does 'sexy' like Helena Christensen, along with her business partner Camilla; their Staerk & Christensen fashion line of undergarments worn as outerwear celebrates the female form.

Yes, underwear is our little secret. A girl's own private castle. Unless you're a 1990s hip-hop chick still wearing your baggies so everyone is privy to your choice in keks, for the most part no one knows what grundies you're sporting, if any at all. Allow me to lift the lid on my personal approach to covering my bits: I'm not really a lingerie girl. I don't own a bra and I'll take a pair of comfy big grandma knickers over a wisp of lace any day. I like my undies wider than dental floss, thank you very much, and I have some choice words for the inventor of the string thong.

That said, I understand the appeal of the world of Coco de Mer or Agent Provocateur: ultrafeminine and sensual in a way that makes most women feel empowered and sexy. Even brands that specialise in more comfortable underwear have looks that suggest you 'didn't make an effort, but girl you're looking fiiiine'.

There is no right or wrong formula to determine which undergarments will fill you with confidence and diablerie; when you want to look your absolute best, wear underwear that makes you feel your best, whether that's shapewear or basic knickers labelled with the days of the week. Give yourself some range: from granny's bloomers to bondage and everything in between. Spanx and corsets that sculpt your shape. The mod range like my sexy Tommy Hilfiger modal set that is simultaneously the *softest* thing I've ever had against my skin and the most flattering set of underwear I own. Casual but f*cking gorgeous.

Certain undergarments in classic fabrics add standout allure when worn as outerwear. This technique is *très* à la mode (and I'm not talking about adding a scoop of vanilla ice cream to a slice of apple pie). Looking trashy is the biggest risk when stepping out in an ensemble featuring visible lingerie. If that's the look you're going for, more power to you. But if you want to express your style in a more subtle but risqué way, you can incorporate slinky smalls and still be the epitome of elegance. A simple sheer top exposing a flattering bra, crop top or corset works like a charm. Build your outfit from the underwear up, making sure everything blends with what you're wearing underneath. This can be achieved with aplomb – from Gwyneth's nightie to Madonna's bustier. The key is to mix it up so you don't look like you just got out of bed or you're halfway through a lap dance.

Classic Under/Outer Combos

- **lingerie** under an **oversized suit**
- a **fancy bra** under a **ripped vintage décolleté shirt** with jeans and a blazer or leather jacket
- **high-waisted Calvin Klein bikini briefs** or **fancy lace knickers** under **low-cut boyfriend jeans**
- a **simple silk slip** worn as a summer dress, dressed down with **Converse**

Helena wearing lingerie from the Staerk & Christensen line.

Couture Gangster

Shalom Harlow is a true original. A prototype badass, this gangster gal oozes swagger, sass and counterculture class. If you were a Canadian kid during the 1990s, it was impossible not to know who she was, as requests for the 'Shalom' replaced Jennifer Aniston's 'Rachel' at hair salons everywhere.

The first time I saw this firebrand in action was on Fashion TV in 1999, during the finale of the Alexander McQueen show where her statuesque frame was being spun around on a turntable-like platform whilst paint was being sprayed on her by robots, à la Jackson Pollock. As you can readily imagine, this cyberpunk-before-cyberpunk-was-a-thing spectacle left an enduring impression on me, kick-starting all manner of magical thoughts and opening countless creative possibilities in my teenage mind.

For me she's one of the most inspirational figures in fashion's rich history and one of the best models to ever place high heel to catwalk. Seemingly unaware of how much she was at the vanguard of change, this genuinely naturalistic kid breathed new life and energy into fashion shoots, arguably reinventing them. She brought edge and character to the creative process through her effortlessly abstract expression and skilled movements.

Shalom's eclectic style covers such a wide range it is difficult to define, but it has a bohemian, spiritual feel to it, with a touch of the New Age. Over the years, she has transformed and adapted her couture frame with an attitude and elegance that could make a duffel bag look good.

She can rock everything from a masculine suit to 1920s flapper attire that complements her classically trained ballerina's physique. She can transport us to the glamour of the red carpet in refined and structural gowns. She lends soul to the clothes she's wearing with presence and personality. Her attitude exudes what modern feminism should ultimately be about: empowerment.

PRO TIP

Like Shalom, choose clothes that represent you and that complete your personality. Choose clothes that you're comfortable in, that make you feel strong and confident. Don't follow trends, don't disappear under a costume. You are the one who can make an outfit shine.

Shalom by Inez &
Vinoodh for *V* magazine,
autumn 2007, issue no. 48.

When I'm good,
I'm very good.
But when I'm bad
I'm even better.

Mae West

Signature Haircut

New Locks, New Looks

Back in the 1990s, Shalom's iconic 1920s-inspired cut made us all frantically run to the hairdressers while quoting Mae West. Going from long to short after a dramatic scissor job at a salon can be daunting. When I chopped my mane off, I cried for a month straight. My hair was my safety blanket, a comforter, a warm safe place where I used to hide and wait for the thunder and the rain to quietly pass me by. For others though, chopping off their curls can feel liberating – a way to announce a new chapter in one's life.

Whatever your reasons, don't be afraid to break old habits, or even drastically change your clothing choices to accommodate your new hairdo.

- **Wear boxy structural garments** (à la Mia Farrow in the 1960s) with a pixie cut.
- **Experiment with big/bold/bulky jewellery**, like hoop earrings or even a black lace choker, which draws attention to your neck line.
- **Give your décolleté a boost** with a great push-up bra when wearing something low cut.

With Shalom in NYC the day we met.

Minimalist

Sweet Carolyn. The archetypal American beauty, the perfect girl next door, wholesome as apple pie, Carolyn Murphy can make an image sing – from iconic *Vogue* covers to those life-altering Gucci shots during the reign of Tom Ford.

This gorgeous concrete blonde with big blue eyes has thirty years at the top of the fashion industry under her belt and, with her flawless complexion, a long-running contract as an Estée Lauder ambassador. Her sense of style is immaculate; this species of perfect woman never delivers any kind of red carpet faux pas. She also has a perfect eye for interior design. And Carolyn is everyone's favourite mum at the PTA meeting.

Her impressive career would be a tad intimidating if she wasn't so approachable and down-to-earth. Carolyn's connection to nature is matched by her willingness to protect it: the environment, the ocean, the planet and all God's creatures that inhabit it. We crossed paths socially and professionally, but our connection developed over environmental work, collaborating when she became a 'No More Plastic' ambassador for my dear friend Rosalie Mann's nonprofit to protect the oceans. Left to her own devices, you'll find her happiest exploring woodlands, working barefoot in her garden or surfing along the Montauk shore.

Carolyn was always joyfully talkative, an exceptional raconteur. Her hilarious anecdotes about the good old days of the industry are carefully doused with the thick syrup of adventure. Conscious of her role as an activist, Carolyn uses her platform, leading by example to effectively encourage positive change.

It's Easy Being Green

Carolyn's effortless beauty and minimalist chic approach make her a perfect case study of sustainability in fashion and the pursuit of an environmentally friendly lifestyle. Considering the effect a purchase will have on the future of our planet and what kind of waste it will create is key. It's sobering, but the time for shrugging and giving up has long gone. As consumers, we have more control over the big clothing companies than we realise. When unified, we can let them know it's important to us by speaking with our wallets. They're smart. They watch what we spend our money on and tailor their product to market demands.

Casual Carolyn by
Dan Martensen.

Cosmetics

It's a tricky business writing overarching advice for makeup and its application, given that everyone's face is different – from skin tone to texture to bone structure, etc. Not to mention the broader context of personal style and taste; makeup is a creative enterprise.

Whenever a professional is doing my makeup, I always ask questions: it's an invaluable opportunity to learn tricks of the trade and they invariably comply, in conspiratorially hushed tones, making me swear to tell no one. I'd love to spill the beans, but they'd kill me. Alternatively, I could, but then I'd have to kill you. Sadly, my publishers insist that readercide is a bad look for a first-time author.

With the personalised application of cosmetics, I can't say it better than 'practice makes perfect'. Trends are constantly changing, so there are no absolutes. For example, eyebrows frame the face – I'm glad we don't pluck them to death any more.

Take a minute to look in the mirror. What features do you consider your strongest? What do you see as problem areas? The point of highlighting and contouring is to draw attention to certain features, and it's safe to say most of us want to highlight cheekbones and bronze cheeks.

When deciding on your evening's war paint, unless you're treading tiles somewhere particularly dim, it's best to choose between dramatic eyes *or* dramatic lips. **Unless you're going on stage, with makeup, it's best not to put a hat on a hat.** Makeup that looks natural has become so ubiquitous that we don't exactly need to be minimalist to be discreet. The trick to applying makeup well is that, at its best, it's hard to tell whether it's being worn at all.

Follow the Leader

The reason youngsters these days are so proficient at applying makeup is, in large part, due to the plethora of tutorial videos available on YouTube. To become more proficient, follow their lead; allow yourself a little time in front of a mirror, armed with some wet-wipes, to play along with a curated selection of videos (try NikkieTutorials, Jeffree Star and Wayne Goss). Learn your eye shape and what suits it. Get to know the topography of your facial bone structure. Most of all though, have fun with it; it's meant to be an enjoyable, creative process. If makeup isn't your thing, or if your skin doesn't react well to cosmetics, keep your makeup regimen as basic and simple as possible.

Fresh-faced Carolyn: less is more.

Rescue Makeup Tips

Your Vanity Essentials

- **MAC Cosmetics Prime Fix+:** to refresh your makeup and obtain a more luminous effect
- **Charlotte Tilbury Full Fat Lashes** black mascara
- **A lash curler**
- **MAC Cosmetics Face and Body foundation:** for a luminous and transparent skin tone; there is a wide range suitable for all skin tones and they come in travel sizes to fit into your makeup bag
- **Eye drops:** essential for perking up your eyes when you've had little sleep
- **Ice Mint chewing gum**
- **YSL Touche Eclat All-Over Brightening Pen:** perfect for touching up your makeup … from the day before

- **Carmex lip balm**
- **Glossier Cloud Paint in 'Puff':** to have pretty pink cheeks, which freshens the complexion, you have to pinch your cheeks – or just add a touch of this blush to your cheekbones
- **Mac Cosmetics Ruby Woo matte lipstick:** so that you're always ready for an unexpected night, a touch of this lipstick will transform your day makeup into a night look. You'll be good to go in thirty seconds!
- **Chanel Blotting Papers:** to remove unwanted shine from your face, plus, the packaging is ultra chic
- And, last but not least, always remember to pack your dark **Ray-Ban Wayfarers** and an **iPhone charger** in case of emergency

`PRO TIP`

It is a crime not to prime. For makeup longevity, the best thing you can do is prime your face to keep everything from moving around.

Carolyn in her
signature jeans.

Go Back to Basics

1 **Avoid 'choice paralysis':** You don't
need to buy a ton of clothes in order to
look good – besides overwhelming your
wardrobe space, when it comes time
to pick the right ensemble for the right
occasion, you won't know where to start.
Instead, invest in a few classic pieces that
will serve you better long-term.

2 **Do your research:** Go the extra
step to seek out companies that use
sustainable materials.

Keep it Simple

Carolyn is the 'less is more' queen; I've never
seen anyone else make the humble jeans and
T-shirt look so chic! The trick is to know how
to combine the right iconic staple items:

• Match a delicate **cashmere jumper** or
vintage T-shirt with a pair of threadbare rock
'n' roll jeans.
• Add the right **belt** (a touch of colour to define
the waist) and a pair of **boots** – you're winning.
• If the weather calls for more, consider a well-
tailored **trench coat**, complemented with
your favourite **bag**.

Perfect Jeans

Find Your Fit

It's a sad day indeed when we are forced to
admit that a favourite pair of jeans is beyond
repair, that the time has come to replace
them. Finding the right jeans is an art form.
Do they make my butt look weird? Do they
sit properly on my waist, or am I looking a bit
Simon Cowell here? The ole 'find your rise'
fiasco: high-rise or low-cut? We've all seen
more than our fair share of waistlines so low
they become 'rise cracks'. My advice? **If your
bum is coming out of your jeans, they're
not the right fit.** There's really only one way
to find your perfect jeans: if at first you don't
succeed, try, and try, and try again until you
find *the ones*. Once you find the right shape, in
the right denim wash, it's pure gold.

Following double page:
Snapshots of runway
birds and friends over
the years: backstage
and candid wild nights
at my flat during Paris
fashion week.

Milla Jovovich by Chris Brenner.

MILLA JOVOVICH

The Song Bird

Her voice is soft and resonant;
when she speaks, you fall
immediately under her spell.

I was struck
with how innately
she seemed to
know her direction
in life … she always
knew exactly where
she needed to be.

MILLA JOVOVICH IS A FIERCE BEAUTY.
Her famous role as the mysterious hippie hottie in the
1990s flick *Dazed and Confused* cemented her as
Generation X's number one crush with her ethereal,
dream-like magnetism. Her voice is soft and resonant,
and when she talks to you, locking those smoky, pool-like eyes on
yours, you fall instantly under her spell. Milla is an artist with the enduring
gift of a child's curiosity, which has fuelled her to explore and experiment
with many diverse creative endeavours throughout her life. She's a joyful,
pensive and delphic soul, one who's successfully kept her personal life
private. When we first met, I was struck with how innately she seemed
to know her direction in life, a path she's walked with precision, poise
and confidence. Enviably, she always knew exactly where she needed to
be throughout her journey.

She became an independent soul very young, finding early fame as
a child actor. By all accounts she was entirely unfazed by the obvious
potential perils of the experience, an attitude that kept her impervious to
the smoke and mirrors that can lead a young woman into the pitfalls of
the fashion industry.

Milla by Paolo Roversi,
taken for her fashion
line in 2006.

NEW YORK BEGINNINGS

Milla and I met fifteen years ago, around the time I arrived in NYC. I didn't know many people yet, so my life was limited primarily to photo shoots and commuting back and forth from Steven Meisel Studio. It was a turbulent time in my life and I was about to be thrust into a new world for which I had yet to decipher the proper rules of engagement. Despite my naivete, I was ambitious and absorbed everything I saw. But I was treading cautiously, as my Spider-sense was telling me the Universe of High Fashion held little compassion for wide-eyed new satellites like me.

Imagine my surprise, as I was eating a pint of Häagen-Dazs on a bus one autumn evening, when Milla called me up on my old flip phone. I just about choked on a macadamia nut when I heard her voice. After I gathered my faculties (such as they are), I managed to decipher that she was inviting me to an awards ceremony, offering to dress me up in her new collection. I stammered gratefully that I'd love to and, as she rang off, I started blinking at my phone in disbelief so long I almost missed my stop.

You have to understand, I grew up watching anything with Milla in it and utterly idolised her. The night of the ceremony, I had to exert a supreme effort not to call her Leeloo Dallas Multipass. That and the fact that she had been an eastern European immigrant child, just like me, contributed to my disbelief and unbridled joy when we became friends. Milla proved to be a positive, gentle and calming influence in my life, at a time when I was anything but.

Our hangs weren't the usual frenetic maelstrom you'd expect in NYC; instead we'd talk or sing songs, or read prose by the fireplace. Bless her, she'd even indulge me and listen to poems I'd written myself. My literary work back then was something of an acquired taste, less actual poems and more the existential diary jottings of a perplexed bird, which I struggled to understand myself. She always helped me find meaning in these streams of consciousness, reminding me to breathe between cascading choruses. With that same kindness, she helped me unpack this baffling new career and move forward with serenity and strength.

I proudly agreed to model for her at the next New York Fashion Week and, in true Milla style, she invited my parents over for breakfast at her house the morning of the show (they still rave on about it to this day!). Milla's fashion line was a melting pot of historical references from the Victorian era to the 1920s, a series of vintage-inspired gowns and summer dresses that Milla and her partner sewed together themselves with rich embroidery textures and the clever use of lace. Their line was created to be accessible to women of any size or age, and was a perfect fusion of historically conventional patterns and more modern, feminine elements. Their work constantly paid homage to the arts, seeking references from literature and film – which was a maverick thing to do at the time – and their shows were a triumph.

Milla by Chris Brenner, taken over the years at home, on the road and on movie sets in NYC and LA.

THE EARTH
IS MY BED
WELCOME
DOWN
TO
Ruby
Lane
SAVE your Soul
FOR life's GAME
eceive me as a Dancing
Monkey

A HAVEN
IN LOS ANGELES

Milla took me under her wing, becoming a confidant and mentor. Her kind gestures have continued over the years, cementing her enduring 'top friend material' position in my heart. When I went to La-La Land (or Tinseltown as cognoscenti call it) for recording sessions with Sean Lennon at the iconic Capitol Records, I was overwhelmed by the city's size, the parties, the valley girl dilemma, the surf dudes and their brazenly awkward obsession with green grass juice. It all gave me vertigo. Milla recognised this instantly and, knowing how important my music was to me, she gave me a quiet space to focus.

Whenever I think about that stay with Milla, I picture a nice summer breeze or a comforting cup of tea. I'd stare at her the way a toddler stares at an ice cream cone. It was (and remains) hard to believe someone so utterly cool exists. She plays guitar and writes her own songs. She is knowledgeable about history, culture and art. Her beautiful house was peppered with books and she had the most amazing collection of vintage clothes I've ever seen. In the morning she practised martial arts, and during that time she taught me about yoga, meditation and the healing benefits of antioxidants in fruit. Topping off this bucket list of my dreams, she even made me her famous macaroni and cheese - to date it's still the best I've ever had. It felt nice to have someone treat me like their little sister. Looking back it was something I had been craving, even if I thought I was invincible, as we all do at that age, I suppose.

Clockwise from top left to bottom right: Milla: moods.
Bottom left: In front of the Hollywood sign on my first trip to LA when I stayed with Milla.

Chateau Marmont

8221 SUNSET BOULEVARD   HOLLYWOOD CALIFORNIA 90046
TELEPHONE (323) 656-1010   FACSIMILE (323) 655-5311

Milla in her apartment in NYC.

Pages 63–65: Milla wearing vintage, styled by me and photographed by Jen Carey for *Rika Magazine*, at Milla's house in LA, 2010.

Vintage Vibe

Past Meets Present

When you find a beautiful vintage piece at a thrift shop or flea market (does anyone else find that term a little unsettling?), do you find yourself breaking into a happy dance, inadvertently yipping 'score!' a little too loudly?

If the answer is 'duh, of course', then, like Milla and me, you've caught the vintage bug. And it will come as no surprise that, for me, digging through a pile of forgotten garments at the dusty end of an old shop and finding a rare gem from the turn of the century (not *this* century, millennials!) that is going to revolutionise my wardrobe is a feeling better then sex.

PRO TIP

I sometimes think that it's worth buying vintage even when it's a little dishevelled or dog-eared. If you're able to sew, you can bring it back to life and give it a personal edge, adding some unique modifications that are exclusive to your personal style. Or, if you're like me and you can't sew a button, safety pins can be a cool/punk alternative way to go.

Vintage

How to Shop Vintage

Anything from the **belle époque** can transform your outfit from basic to iconic in the blink of an eye. The trick is to consider any vintage garment as the pièce de résistance; it's your main course. Everything else is a side dish.

1 **The Statement Piece:** You can easily wear a vintage piece on its own and allow its uniqueness to shine. If you're wearing a Victorian jacket complete with epaulettes, meticulously embroidered silk and lace, you might not need any additional bells and whistles.

2 **Something Old, Something New:** This old adage isn't just for brides! Go maverick and combine your vintage find with more modern fare, like Milla does. Her fantastic collection would get any vintage enthusiast in a flap, but it's the fresh way she blends vintage with simple modern everyday pieces that we're going to steal. Mix it with a simple jean and T-shirt and add a discreet trainer (I said discreet, guys! Day-Glo Air Jordans should sit this one out).

3 **Avoid the Time Warp:** Too much vintage can make you look a little ridiculous, too. If you find yourself leaving the house in a full corset and petticoat combination, liberally besprinkled with a bonnet and frilly parasol, there's a chance that you may have gilded the lily a trifle, so don't be surprised if you get mistaken for Mary Poppins (even if we all secretly think that she is supercalifragilisticexpialidocious).

Kate Moss by Alasdair McLellan for *Vogue* Paris, October 2011.

KATE MOSS

Muse of a Thousand Faces

Dear Kate,

It was the way you smoked your cigarette
that always fascinated me.

The secret of Kate's longevity has
a lot to do with her avant-garde attitude, originality and fearless sense of style.

KATE MOSS IS AN ENIGMA who has intrigued millions of people around the world for more than three decades. Initially considered an atypical beauty, that concept went out the window when a scientific study showed her facial features and symmetrical bone structure fit a mathematical equation that calculates the dimensions of the quintessential, perfect beauty.

Her distinctive 'waif' look (echoing Twiggy's 1960s silhouette) revolutionised the world of fashion in the early 1990s, but it was arguably her chameleon-like versatility that has made her a household name throughout the years. I reckon the secret of Kate's longevity has a lot to do with her avant-garde attitude, originality and fearless sense of style. The right girl at the right time, this quiet kid from Croydon shook the mainstream to its very foundations, while maintaining a secretly subversive punk sensibility.

With meteoric fire, Kate became a global style icon. Despite giving very few interviews, her charismatic personality galvanised the press. Her capacity to inspire, project and reflect in every image was unprecedented. She can tell a whole story with a look in her eyes, courageously bearing her truth and, ultimately, reflecting yours. No easy task! But Kate makes it look easy. As you can imagine, for the brands lucky or savvy enough to work with her, this is a priceless quality in a model.

Throughout the years, I've seen her anticipate fashion trends and predict their direction. Not only within the industry, but also on the streets – something the business often gets preposterously wrong. She operates instinctively through intuition. Either that, or the girl's got a secret time machine that she ain't sharing!

To paint in primary colours: Kate is a straight-up gangster. In an age of information overload ad nauseam, she has forever remained a singular, mysterious entity. She's the muse of a thousand faces. She's a fiercely independent inspiration to millions of women who relate to something intangible they see in Kate. Fame and notoriety can come at a price though, and she's no stranger to controversy and heartbreak. It's a cruel irony that celebrity can at times become a kind of prison; the more people know your name, the lonelier it can be. That said, Kate is one of the strongest people I've ever known.

Kate Moss in New York
at a Fashion Week event
in Bryant Park, 1995.

FASHION
WEEK WARRIOR

At the end of my first fashion week season, I remember trying to get myself together to make it down the long and winding Ritz Paris corridor to seek sanctuary in Kate's room. I was convinced that everyone else was out to kill me.

   I dragged my deflated spirit and bony carcass to her floor, but after exiting the lift, my progress literally slowed to a crawl. As her room number lurched into view above me, I banged my fist as hard as I could on the base of the wooden door.

   It swung open, revealing Miss Moss: radiant as sunlight, wearing her signature skinny jeans, a decadent Balenciaga top and a pair of Native American moccasins. Defying physics by somehow simultaneously sipping a beer and taking a drag on a cigarette, she looked quizzically at the empty space where my head and shoulders should have been. Following the stertorous sound of my breathing, her eyes met mine, which, seconds before, had been inspecting the stitching of her moccasins.

KATE
Rini, WTF?
(*without missing a beat,
dropping down to hug me*)
What happened?

ME
(*crying, as soon as I hear Kate's voice*)
I don't know how the hell you do this.
I can't. . . . This fashion thing is insane.
I quit. . . . I'm not built for it.

KATE
(*helping me to my feet, manoeuvring my head
until I was looking straight into her eyes, and
speaking soothingly, but firmly*)
Another model tried to strangle
me my first season. So you get yourself
together and you get back to work.

Not for the first time, nor for the last, 'Florence Katingale' swung into action. After eight hours of sleep and some overpriced spaghetti, I got back in line and did as I was told.

   Kate was my mentor during the first years of my career. Truth be told, I could never have asked for a better fairy godmum to guide me through the intricate maze, the disorientating hall of mirrors, that is the fashion industry.

Candid shots with Kate, playing dress up
during a shoot for Kate's first Topshop collection, London, 2006.

Changement de rôle.

JUNGLE JAM

During the summer of 2006, I joined Kate and Mick Jones (The Clash, Big Audio Dynamite) in Bali for a month of epic adventures and jungle fun. This was to be a fashionable holiday, so I packed my best boho chic summer dresses and 1970s-inspired ensembles, while of course forgetting to pack one single swimming costume. One of my favourite aspects of travelling with Kate was that I'd get to borrow her clothes. We'd often play dress-up, mixing and matching the contents of our suitcases. Watching her put an outfit together was mesmerising: clothes bundled on the bed or festooned on the floor in a carnival of texture and colour (picture Liza Minnelli ravaging her room in *Cabaret* or the shirt scene in *The Great Gatsby*).

I arrived bright-eyed and bushy-tailed to our Indonesian hippy sanctuary, brandishing an old Underwood typewriter, a copy of *Les Poètes Maudits* (to be devoured on the beach) and as many packs of cigarettes as I could cram into my luggage.

I'd barely set my bags down before Kate informed me that my presence had been requested at a formal dinner that evening, so would I mind terribly going to snatch a swift shower and slipping into something a little less comfortable?

Memories from Bali include hide-and-seek with the kids, a renewed love for half-forgotten songs, sunburns and mimosas by the beach, epic storytelling sessions in the tree house, fierce historical debates and drunken battles around the chessboard with Mick.

One morning, Mr Jones came face to face with a venomous cobra that had taken up residence underneath our beach house. As the coiled contender stared down this mild-mannered, self-educated, working-class West London eccentric who insisted on wearing a cardigan in the tropical heat, it failed to realise that, in fact, there stood a punk legend who can rewrite a singer's lazy middle eight at 100 yards. Mick (my hero) had not only survived being in a band with Joe Strummer, he had also produced three records with Peter Doherty at the height of the latter's eating-squirrels-and-sticking-straw-in-his-hair lunacy.

After momentarily mistaking the uninvited guest for Nick Kent, Jonsey maintained his composure during this Mexican standoff. A distant church bell chimed. Unwavering stares narrowed to a squint. A few reverb-drenched harmonica notes echoed menacingly.

The cobra drew first.

Without warning, the huge snake lurched forward. Mick — with agility that belied both his age and his cardigan — seized the broomstick he had placed in the garden to fend off any local fauna that took a shine to his breakfast egg. With the same fearlessness Mick displays when he tells a lead guitarist that a song doesn't, strictly speaking, need a solo, he lunged at his assailant and pinned it to the floor just below the head, which was hissing in surprise and protest. Mick slackened the downward pressure and unleashed a primordial bellow the likes of which have not been heard since he toured *London Calling*. Wisely sensing he'd met his match, the cobra scarpered off, taking refuge in a giant vase at the bottom of the garden.

Now, here's the thing: if this had happened to me, I would have certainly died. My heart would have stopped beating right there on the spot. Which is why no one told me about it until we were safely on board the plane headed to the island of Java (which, I was reassured in the calmest of tones, had been cleared of all snakes prior to our arrival).

Travel memories from Bali in August 2006 featuring Kate, Lily and Mr Jones.

The ancient Buddhist temple of Borobudur, nestled in Java's gorgeous and dense jungle, is one of the most staggeringly beautiful structures in the world. Adding to the mystique was the arrival of my dear friend Lily Cole who joined our party of intrepid explorers, a beautiful young woman whose brain is the size of a planet.

We set out at 3 am in order to catch the sunrise over the top of the world's largest Buddhist temple. But before we did, there was a brief hiccup to the plan as we experienced an existential fashion crisis. None of us could decide on the right outfit for this spiritual expedition. Mick endeavoured to lend some rational perspective: surely it didn't really matter what we wore as we hacked our way through the undergrowth. One of the distinguishing features of the jungle, he argued, was a conspicuous absence of press, photographers or indeed any kind of human civilisation. Furthermore, he reasoned — with heroic restraint in his tone — neither the guides nor their elephants would notice if an Azzedine Alaia silk dress was ruined by the Galliano belt, nor if the Philip Treacy hat was a shade too gaudy with that outfit (this later turned out to be questionable advice; I saw the judge-y side-eye my elephant gave my ensemble). Mercifully we all agreed that 6-inch McQueen heels were not the best choice for this particular jungle exploration, as we may wish to save those for climbing Mount Everest.

Lily joined me to offer moral support, but in doing so the process soon turned into a couture fitting where all the world's designers had to be included lest they feel left out. When Kate said to Lily, 'Oh I know, get the Chanel; Karl would love this', it became clear that it was too early to effectively shine any common sense on the proceedings, and surely my case for the jeans and T-shirt option sounded ridiculous. The following hour became an Italian *Vogue* exposé that would have made Franca Sozzani reach for the popcorn. An animated exchange about Marc Jacobs's use of patterns and sculpted shapes in his latest collection and Alber Elbaz's use of bright colours at Lanvin followed. Then the absurdity of the moment overcame me and I blurted 'Guys! We're going to a f*cking temple!' To which Kate calmly replied, 'Keep your hat on, Rini. Of course there'll be paparazzi following us.'

I paused and considered the likelihood of a newspaper paying a morally corrupt photographer to follow a model halfway across the planet to crouch in the Javanese jungle on the off-chance of snapping not the endangered Javan rhino, but the lesser-spotted Croydonian cutie. It seemed too surreal a proposition to process. Eventually we agreed to disagree and I breathed a sigh of relief as she finally slipped on a pair of jeans and a T-shirt before we began our adventure. As soon as we set out, we noticed a flash of paparazzi lurking in the underbrush, devoid of camouflage or dignity. 'Told you so, Reens!', Kate fluted as the sound of camera shutters blended with the chatter of the thronging insects. We shook our heads, laughing, and pressed on.

Sunrise over the Borobudur Temple in Java
and travels with Kate and Lily.

The Chameleon

Kate is a bona fide style icon. Her nonchalant and effortless energy breathes authenticity and sensuality.

While history may not credit Kate with actually inventing rock 'n' roll chic, she incarnated and amplified it to the point where you'd be forgiven for assuming she had. In every frame committed to celluloid, she exudes an irresistible attitude that says 'Hi. I woke up like this. I know I look hot. I clearly don't care if you agree.' And we quietly concede; this unspoken dialogue between beauty and the beholders is universally uncontested.

Her every jagged silhouette, recycled from discarded designer duds, carries a story – one that evokes an iconic image we half remember. She assembles looks like a prodigal musician who innately understands harmony. Kate sees symmetry where we see missing sequins. She sees next summer's season where we see moth-eaten moccasins. Secondhand to her has never been second-best.

Famously a sartorial chameleon, Ms Moss had the benefit of studying for many years under fashion's greatest luminary designers, though she instinctively knew how to project their specific aesthetic. Given this constant assault on the senses, a lesser mortal might understandably have lost a sense of their own personal style. But a strong individual fashion sense comes as a result of a strong personality, not vice versa. And Kate's is bulletproof. Upon inspection, this is true for all of the most iconic girls. When she's not getting paid to get dressed, her own style hasn't changed much over the last three decades: haute couture with a side of delinquency. Punk rock via thrift shop piracy. Pink might make the boys wink, but Kate makes high street retail think.

Above: Kate at the 1995 Costume Institute Gala.

Facing page: Kate arriving at a party for John Waters's film *Serial Mom*, NYC, 1994.

Some people have
the capacity
to change the air
in a room when
they enter it.

How to Make an Entrance

Some people have the capacity to change the air in a room when
they enter it. Kate is the master. She'll hypnotise you with charm and
charisma; she'll play DJ and guess your favourite song; she'll get the
party started by changing into an outfit made from rags and curtains;
she'll get you dancing faster than you can wiggle your nose or call your
mama to tell her you're not coming home tonight.

What's even more impressive is the fact that she appears to have
learned how to turn this panache on and off as if on tap. To illustrate:
I've seen her cross a crowded restaurant undetected, unrecognised,
apparently transparent and inexplicably invisible, to arrive at her table,
sit down next to me and say, with a mischievous twinkle in her eye,
'And now for my next trick: Kate is gonna *Arrive*.'

Laughing and shaking my head, I watched as she stood up and
made her way back to the entrance undetected. A moment later, re-
entering and wearing exactly the same clothes, the transformation was
unbelievable. Her body and energy tapered and snapped. Somehow,
now everyone *saw* her. Even people who hadn't spotted her yet looked
up from their filets mignons, wondering if the music had just got louder.
She took the same route through the tables, and still hadn't spoken a
word. But while seconds before she had passed through like a ghost,
on this second take, the whole restaurant was gasping and trying to
maintain composure. The women watched soundlessly as the men
straightened their ties. I rolled my eyes as she sat down next to me for
the second time, and we both laughed into our bread rolls.

Kate making an entrance
vs the French exit,
aka an Irish goodbye.

Leopard Print + It-Bag

Copy Kat

Stay true to your style when incorporating trends:

1 Kate Moss's style conjures up a precise silhouette: oversized coat, mini dress or skirt, fabulous ballerina flats or sexy high boots and brilliant accessories like maxi-sunglasses and a **billion-dollar handbag** carried as nonchalantly as possible.

2 She's wild about **animal prints**.

3 Mossy is an intuitive stylist with impeccable taste. She dares to bring back classics by **mixing vintage with current fashion trends**.

4 She is not afraid to take risks. She often plays a game by flipping the codes; she **dresses up for a casual gathering** at the pub and **dresses down while still exuding simple elegance on the red carpet**.

5 She knows how to play to her strengths and chooses clothes with **the right structure and fit** for her body type.

6 She is loyal to her **signature look** and to her **favourite designer friends**.

Facing page: Kate sporting her signature spots in NYC.

Above: Kate with a show-stopping It-bag in London.

The Glastonbury Look

What to Wear to a Festival

Preparing for the Glastonbury Festival takes planning, multitasking in the face of destabilising challenges and the full deployment of one's wits and concentration to achieve a higher state of consciousness . . . through one iconic, effortless look.

Choosing the right outfit is key, as you are entering into the fashionista's survival-of-the-fittest arena. You have to be stylish while being practical, warm and dry. Not easy when one is off their nut.

The relationship between music and fashion has always been a match made in heaven: music as a healing force and a means of communication, and fashion as a way of expressing one's identity and creating a sense of belonging through a kind of uniform or armour. Stolen moments at Glastonbury are captured in timeless photographs that have culturally defined entire generations. There is a fine line between *Fantasia* and the imaginary world of costume creation, transforming rags into high-end craftsmanship.

When you think of festival fashion, particularly Glastonbury, your mind probably flashes to Kate's iconic looks throughout the years. I know mine does. The gold mini dress, black leather belt and muddy wellies from 2005 (she smashed it!). There's something intangibly magical about that image. Most of us think we'd look ridiculous if we tried to pull off that outfit; like we'd narrowly escaped the jaws of death as an extra from a John Carpenter film, surviving a car crash in the swamps of the Bayou whilst being chased by a disturbed (yet strangely good-looking) serial killer.

That image has something that you can't copy, steal or buy. It's got charisma.

If necessity is the mother of invention, then despair must be the mother of last-resort innovation. That outfit was created on a whim the very same morning. Kate had originally planned to wear a long gown that day, but it had been raining for forty-eight hours; if you've ever been to Glastonbury when it's been raining for more than two hours, you'll know this option was out the window. Unfazed, Kate grabbed a pair of scissors and unwittingly reinvented rock chic standards. When you look at that photograph, you can smell the authenticity, the debauchery, the glorious and joyous chaos of that day. It's irresistible, but we don't know exactly why. Hmm … I just can't explain it. Maybe it's the reminiscence of a fabulous and fun time – if only any of us could remember.

Peter Doherty and Kate at the Glastonbury Music Festival at Worthy Farm, Pilton, in Somerset, UK, 25 June 2005.

FF·1 2010 TX

Clockwise from top left: Festival style inspiration from a shoot in London in 2004 (far left) and photographs by François Rotger include an Italian *Marie Claire* editorial from October 2008 and three personal photographs.

My Festival Survival Tips

Now, to be honest, I'm not exactly well placed to dole out basic advice or educate you on proper etiquette at a music festival: my first time at Glasto, I woke up in the middle of a muddy field wearing an orange jumpsuit, sporting only one welly and unable to spell my own name. Maybe it would be best if, instead, I tell you guys what *not* to do.

1 Whatever you do, DO **NOT** FORGET to bring toilet paper.

2 Carry a piece of paper with your name, your mates' phone numbers (seven people at the festival plus three besties in the country who are likely to be sober) and a bunch of Polaroids that can help you retrace your steps. This is a practical tip in case you get hit with a sudden case of amnesia.

3 Don't forget to install the 'find my phone' app and to share your location with your temporary legal guardian. If you're anything like me, they'll use it to locate you after you've been MIA for more than forty-eight hours, still telling yourself it's Friday, when some well-informed Good Samaritan helpfully points out that it's *Sunday afternoon*.

4 Stop drinking at noon (morning drinking is only to combat hangovers), then don't start again till the sun sets. Don't pass out drunk in the sun! You might wake up with the worst sunburn of your life. Mud should not be considered an effective sunscreen.

5 Don't pass out in a stranger's tent; you might wake up cuddling a weird individual named Uncle Bobby.

6 Make sure to bring all your over-the-counter pharmaceuticals; if you rely on the local pharmacy dispenser, you could end up with fake aspirin and bad antihistamine.

7 Bring your own reusable water bottle and keep yourself hydrated while reducing the plastic pollution that is destroying our environment.

Above: A festival outfit.

Facing page: My first professional photograph, taken by Jan Welters the day I arrived in Paris, January 2002.

Curate Your Own
Rock 'n' Roll Attitude

Pages 88–89: Kate in Prada by Luigi & Iango for *Vogue* Hong Kong, March 2021.

- Pay attention to your movements and gestures: **flip off** as many strangers as you can.
- Be conscious of your body posture: **slouch** as much as possible.
- Learn how to play with the intensity of your look: if you don't **scare away innocent bystanders**, you're doing it wrong.
- Don't overdo it with hair and makeup; **less is more**.
- **Don't brush your hair.**
- **Sleep in your mascara** for three nights in a row.

Karl's brigade, Paris 2006,
photographed by William Klein for *Harper's Bazaar*.

CHANEL FOREVER

In fashion, you always have
to break something to make it again,
to love what you've hated
and hate what you've loved.

Karl Lagerfeld

From eccentric muses to world travel and a fierce love of history, Karl found a way to transform every moment into lyrical, avant-garde garments.

MY STYLE WAS FORGED BY A HANDFUL OF KEY INDIVIDUALS who shook my previous misconceptions inside out. Elegant artists who left their mark on our generation by shaping silhouettes and minds.

It's an odd truth that the range of 'appropriate' styles readily available to us are specific to an occasion or even a time of day. The odds improve as we approach the evening, and get even better late at night. Once we're past the bedtime of constricting societal standards, that range broadens wildly and we can be as odd and peculiar as we wish. And folks, Karl Lagerfeld was a night owl.

His prolific creativity knew no bounds. This man got more done in a single day than most do in a lifetime.

I saw him as a contemporary poet, seeking inspiration from every corner of his life. From eccentric muses to world travel and a fierce love of history, Karl found a way to transform every moment into lyrical, avant-garde garments. With a loving nostalgia for the artistic crafts of the belle époque and the legacy left by Coco Chanel, he seemed to constantly reinvent himself. Lagerfeld drew from the past whilst remaining achingly current, setting the tone, styles and trends for the ever-changing seasons.

He was a perfectionist who excelled at anything to which he turned his fingerless gloves. Karl would surround himself with talented people; he gifted them guidance, freedom and, crucially, the confidence to triumph in their craft. An impressive judge of character, too, he saw through people and encouraged them to be the best version of themselves. Karl had a brilliant nose for recognising talent and was unafraid of taking a chance with someone, going on little more than instinct.

Knowledge was his passion; he taught me everything I know about fashion and art. For his work, he would repeatedly find a story, a narrative within every photograph, every collection. He was a world builder. And every universe his beautiful mind conjured up created a feeling of raw emotion in people. He was a master storyteller who celebrated eccentricity, as long as it remained chic.

I loved how he hated mediocrity, it bored him. Blessed with a subtle, dry sense of humour, he remained a loyal and unique creature of habit with boundless curiosity: 'Karl and everything chic: a love story'.

In the finale wedding dress with Karl during Chanel's F/W 2006–7 Couture show in Paris.

FROM RUE CAMBON TO THE CATWALK

When I arrived in Paris in the early 2000s, the models who succeeded in fashion looked nothing like me. They were beautiful, tall, with legs that went on for days. I looked like Cousin It.

The beginning of my career proved to be a brutal test of perseverance. I had such a distinctive look that no one could figure out what to do with me. I didn't fit in with any of the norms of what a model should look like at the time. I was too short, too weird, my nose was crooked and I had way too much hair. I must've had a thousand doors slammed in my face before one opened, but it only takes one, and that door led to Karl Lagerfeld and Chanel.

As I entered Rue Cambon for my first Chanel casting I stumbled into a morass of dozens of models, all drop-dead stunning. My heart sank. I waited for three hours before it was my turn. After the preliminary Polaroids I was expecting them to send me on my merry way. To my great surprise however, they took me to meet Virginie Viard, then the studio director. Virginie is an attentive, charismatic and gentle soul and for some reason she took an immediate liking to me. 'She looks like a doll,' I remember her saying before she dressed me herself in one of the outfits and took me to meet the Kaiser himself.

Now, technically speaking, a model isn't supposed to speak during these proceedings.

The code of conduct dictates silence, discretion and grace. Unfortunately none of my strongest assets! When I get nervous, I babble. Within seconds of entering his presence, the butterflies had me performing a monologue of such profound nonsense that Bridget Jones and Ally McBeal would have both been shuffling their feet and elbowing me in the ribs.

The surprise of my strong French Canadian accent may have worked in my favour by making me seem provincially charming. Thankfully, Karl found the whole scene amusing. 'I like her,' he proclaimed. 'She reminds me of Juliette Gréco. But that accent has got to go!'

I didn't know it then, but that moment changed my life forever.

Soon I was a fixture at most major Chanel events, fashion shows and photo shoots. For the first time I felt like I belonged, that I was part of a team. I would frequently visit them au studio. I loved witnessing the creation of the collection. The whole process was mesmerising, how a beautiful sketch that Karl imagined would be transformed into a gorgeous garment to appear on the runway — the amazing craftsmanship of the seamstresses, the meticulous embroidery, the elaborate fittings where everyone would frantically run around adding the last details to create that iconic Chanel look.

Clockwise from top left,
Backstage at the Chanel F/W 2007–8 RTW show;
two photographs from the Chanel Métiers d'Art 'Paris-Monte Carlo' 2006–7 collection press kit
and a candid shot in a dress from the collection; with Karl in Miami for a private Chanel dinner.

Accessoires: Studio **CHANEL** – Paris

Couture réalisée par: Odile Gilbert

Maquillage: **CHANEL**

Son – Stylist: Michel Gaubert

Mention obligatoire **CHANEL** – Photo Karl Lagerfeld
Obligatory mention **CHANEL** – Photo Karl Lagerfeld

Model – Déposée Registered Model

Reproduction et/ou cropping forbidden

This print is made with stochastic-screening reproduce your photographic year high print without screen pattern

Service de Presse 29/31 Rue Cambon 75 Paris Tel. 01
E-mail: presse.mode@chanel-corp.com

More imperfections
are heard in chaos and noise
than in moments
of stillness and quiet.
But beauty isn't perfect.
It's in the lines
of a well-worn smile
and the uncertainties of our flaws.

...

Ultimately my favourite memories were from the time I spent with Karl himself. He embraced my quirky style and weird sense of humour. I could've spent a lifetime listening to his stories. We'd talk for hours about history, art and music — from endless exchanges on obscure 1920s short films to unsung German punk bands. I'd bring my journals and write poetry as he sat with regal poise, sketching. He introduced me to the most fascinating books, like *The Marchesa Casati*, and opened my eyes to the rich and fabulous universe of the Roaring Twenties. I learned about characters who changed the course of history with the courage to lead an authentic life back when freedom of expression was considered a crime.

Karl taught me to see beyond the ordinary, to embrace the weird element, because in that detail lies something greater than perfection. Therein we find the truth.

The morning of my first Chanel show I arrived at the venue five hours before the start of the défilé (honest). I was excited, nervous and felt a little out of place. During my fitting someone eventually pointed to the elephant in the room — I was clearly too short for this particular outfit. Karl simply shrugged and said, 'Well, cut the dress then.' Compounding my paranoia about being a tad vertically challenged in the company of the show's six-foot plus models in high heels, they decided to fit me in ballet flats.

I could feel my heart beating through my ribcage as I stepped onto the runway, pausing to shoot a glance at Karl, a look he correctly interpreted as 'you sure about this?' He held my hands with a kind but firm grasp and said, '*C'est facile.* Now you walk.'

Clockwise from top left,
Chanel F/W 2006–7 Couture show, performing at the Chanel Métiers d'Art 'Paris-London' 2007–8 show;
Virginie Viard photographed in Gabrielle Chanel's apartment at 31 Rue Cambon in Paris.

CHANEL
PARIS-MONTE CARLO 2006

CHANEL – Paris

apeaux ar : Maison Michel
Bijoux par : Desrues
Broder s par : Lesage
es par : Massaro

r: Odile Gilbert
CHANEL

Modèle Déposé – Reg Mod

Recadrage interdit – Cro ing forbidd

This print is made with stochastic-s
high-quality-scan from this print

Service de Presse 29/31 Rue Cambon 75001 Paris – Tel. : 01 42 86 28 00
E-mail: presse.mode@chanel-corp.com

Karl loved girls with personality. Strong women never frightened him; he loved them.

The attitude embodied by a model on the catwalk is essential to bringing the right mood to the garment; it can give it life. Karl loved girls with personality. Strong women never frightened him; he loved them. I recall being told many times by people in his entourage never to betray any vulnerability in his company, nor should I display sadness or raw emotion, as he'd consider it a sign of weakness. Nothing was further from the truth, at least in my experience. I found him to be a person who celebrated honesty.

One of my most vivid memories with Mr Lagerfeld occurred during a cover shoot for *Visionaire* magazine. Karl's idea was to transform me into Anna de Noailles, a Romanian countess from the turn of the century. Most of Karl's shoots took place at night, and I had just arrived from LA after my fourth transatlantic journey that week. I was utterly exhausted and close to a breakdown.

The moment I stepped on set, Karl noticed how frail I was. The truth is I was fighting back tears in the makeup chair.

Assessing the situation, he told the team to take a break, leaving the two of us to take tea in the garden. Stepping outside, we found a spot and sat in silence for a while. The fresh air allowed me to catch my breath and, as I closed my eyes, I felt tears running down my face. He could have said anything, as it was always the tone of his voice with which he truly communicated. But as it happens all he said, softly, was 'are you ok?' I apologised and nodded my head. Speech hadn't quite returned. Like a lullaby on the breeze I heard his voice telling me to breathe. That it was all going to be ok. That this is what I do, that I'm jolly well good at it. Flattered, I shyly sipped my tea and I heard a bashful laugh escape the bashful smile that was slowly replacing my sighs and tears.

It was a human moment. A moment where a great man showed me great kindness and compassion. As we walked back towards the team he paused for a beat, and squeezing my hand said, 'Wipe your tears. Don't ever let them see you cry.'

Clockwise from top left, Transformed into Romanian Countess Anna de Noailles by Karl for the cover of the 1910 portfolio in *Visionaire*, no. 49, 'Decades,' 2006; a scrapped snapshot from a Chanel shoot in 2004; backstage at the Grand Palais for the Chanel S/S 2013 RTW show.

Colour Me

Now I'm sliding, it's intriguing
So young yet too old to learn
That summer is the thirst
The river always runs dry first

You're in heaven
This is heaven now
Was real now

As the light
And the
Wit

The

You're
This is heaven
You're in heaven

Substance
don't resemble
when you
Did

A little's less alarming
In need of some substance
The sun might set
Tonight could be the night
And if thats the case
You'll get on all right
But there's no point
spotting for a fight

In Winter Chill

When all is said and done
So weak and overcome
So tired of running still
The winter

I look into your eyes
An eyelid without sun
Some things you can't disguise
So many people so lonely inside

waiting
And if all this brings you down
I will be coming round

When useless dreaming comes to an end
Who will carry all your fears?

When all the tears from fury have passed
Maybe love has just begun

Like a faded photograph
A child caught in a storm
Though we will never sleep
The winter

There's lipstick on the glass
The questions left unasked
Two fools who've left the game
Finding themselves without solace again

waiting
And if all this brings you down
I will be coming round

When useless dreaming comes to an end
Who will carry all your fears?

When all the tears from fury have passed
Maybe love has just begun

Maybe love has just begun

Because we're blinded by
The darkest ray of light

Performance

Clouded stars that the future will send
And the broken nights that only time will mend
Eternity cannot fade the truth
That nothing is what the hunger is feasting on

I can, you can try

Mo' Pop

You travel through my blood coursing through my veins
And today, the memory like a shadow I can't shake

[French verse]

I confess you've got a hold on me
But I never fall this easily

Your history seems to shroud you like a plague
And you wonder why this thought keeps you awake

I never asked you to step inside my skin
I let you stay here haunting me within

[French verse]

I confess you've got a hold on me
But I never fall this easily

We're real science
We're real science ...

Look into my eyes for the last
You read my lips
love over time

Look into my eyes for th
in you read my lips
You're over

Its growth, not birth
You're one down
But I'm standing
From over here
You look complete

Bleeding faster.....

been basking in the summer sun
I turn the radio on

round me

been basking in the summer sun
I turn the radio on

round me

happen
know that this is real
now that this is real
feel you know that this is real
feel I know that this is real

these things happen
these things happen

Strung Out

Tonight, going to
Pulling me through that open door
Inhibitions dissipate
Now the line's disintegrating
I'm too close to the wire
All strung out on desire
But I'm still there
By your side
On your mind
And in your eyes
The sky's might turn out for you
That's something we'll make true
Regrets beckon like they did before
Pulling me through that open door
Inhibitions dissipate
Now my mind's disintegrating
Tonight something's got to give
Pulling me through that open door

Lover

How can we teach what we do not know
How can we shine when we do not glow
We're losing more than we ever found
We're trying to cros uncovered ground
Now I've seen the other side
I've seen things I just can't hide
How can this die when it's never grown
How can we feel what we've ever found
We're losing more than we ever found
We're trying to uncovered ground

How to Rock a Little Black Dress

Black has long been considered a nostalgic or melancholic colour – for expressing grief in a time of mourning or evoking a certain poetic Victorian sensibility.

Gabrielle Chanel created the first little black dress as early as the 1910s. In 1926, *Vogue* nicknamed the innovative design 'the Chanel "Ford" dress, the frock that all the world will wear.' Her motivation was to design a neutral-coloured garment to be at once revolutionarily chic, yet affordable to all. Due to its simple form and effortless elegance it soon became an essential piece in every woman's wardrobe. One aspect of its genius was to use femininity and elegance to rebel and shake off the shackles of patriarchal bondage. You see, until this point most ensembles involved corsets, stitched-in ribbing and such. With just a small amount of material Coco was actually making a bold statement about the fabric of modern society.

When it comes to self-expression, the LBD was and remains incredibly versatile. You can choose to embellish it with a combination of accessories, or simply wear it as is. Consider it a little black canvas on which to paint your own voice, however bold or bashful it may be.

For such an apparently simple dress, we see it centre stage in many iconic images – from Audrey Hepburn's *Breakfast at Tiffany's* sleek Givenchy to Princess Diana's post-divorce, sexy revenge number. This dress is so versatile you can go from breakfast straight to your divorce trial without batting a smoky eyelid. Or – speaking from experience – directly from a night club to a crucial business meeting. Which reminds me, the little black dress looks great with sunglasses.

From the Chanel S/S 2007 RTW collection press kit, photographed by Karl Lagerfeld.

The Little Black Dress

The 1960s Baby Doll Look

The pop art movement made for a compelling and colourful time in fashion history. Graphic details defined the era, but it also resurrected the little black cocktail dress, which was typically worn until it fell apart and then recycled and restyled in a different way. The black dress resurged in the 1960s, worn in its purest form celebrating its graphic structure and then transformed into a mini-skirt version of the original.

Make it chic: To turn the conventional black dress into a seriously sophisticated statement, remember that the devil is in the detail. A classic and simple piece like the LBD will always draw attention to your face, so your skincare regimen and makeup choices are as important as your accessories.

Now gals, when aiming for a **glowing complexion**, you gotta put in the work:
- Drink loads of **water.**
- Eat your **vegetables**.
- Aim for 7–8 hours of **sleep**.
- This may seem a little 'holistic', but **meditating** really helps. The stress of our daily battles shows up on our face. If meditation ain't for you, **yoga** works as well.
- Here's the annoying bit: Drink **less booze** and **quit smoking**. In other words, do as I say, not as I do.

Above and facing page:
From the Chanel
S/S 2007 RTW
collection press kit,
photographed by
Karl Lagerfeld.

Details, Details, Details

- A head-to-toe black look is a statement you can embellish with a **simple belt** to enhance your waistline, accessorising with anything from a delicate **string of pearls** (fake ones are pretty convincing these days) to **shimmering costume jewellery** around a strappy neckline.
- Nail the look with a classic 'look at me' **red lipstick** and a pair of **pointed-toe black heels** to show off those legs, creating a classically sleek silhouette.
- Add a **Chanel clutch** and you're good to go.
- Optional: **metal cigarette case** or a **perfumed vintage handkerchief**.

The 1990s Grunge Era

The savvy corners of the fashion industry have always kept one eye on the streets. The obscure corners of subculture have always been where trends evolve authentically, forever one step ahead of the designers. This food chain was brought into sharp relief during the 1990s, and the kids caught a glimpse of the wizard behind the curtain. What we were once ridiculed for wearing to Mudhoney gigs began appearing nine months later on runways and magazine covers. What happened with the little black dress during this time illustrates the phenomenon beautifully. While the burgeoning appeal of the rock 'n' roll take on the LBD had been quietly gathering momentum at clubs and gigs, it really came into its own when bands like Sonic Youth, L7 and Babes in Toyland breathed life and anarchy into feminism, making it beautiful, grotesque, irreverent and exciting. The audacious pairing of combat boots or Converse with Coco's iconic black dress offended the sensibilities of the old guard, and we liked it. We weren't thrilled when our vibe got appropriated by the mainstream, but we weren't surprised. We made that sh*t look good.

Channelling Coco's
rebellious spirit in NYC
in a sequin LBD with
a leather jacket.

Make It Edgy
and Cool

Cutting a grunge silhouette in an LBD from Superfine by Lucy Pinter.

A hypothetical yet realistic scenario:

1 You just woke up beside a guy you met in a bar last night. You can't remember his name and he's messed up your hair. Ideally he's cute so you're not considering chewing off your arm rather than waking him before your walk of shame home.

2 You catch your reflection in a mirror. Your hair looks like you're in Mötley Crüe and your mascara's run so far down your face you look like you can give Kiss a run for their money. You wince self-consciously as you step outside. My advice, here, is don't waste your energy. There's no point in hating on yourself when everybody else on the street will do it for you.

3 By the time you get home you may be tempted to wash your face or comb your hair. Or, depending on your religious upbringing, sit in the shower gently sobbing 'unclean … unclean …' to yourself. Do NOT touch anything (OK, absolutely do **brush your teeth**). This is the perfect opportunity to throw on that little black dress you've had hanging in the back of your wardrobe all those years. If you're in London go break hearts in Dalston. If you're in NYC go set fire to Bed-Stuy. If you're in LA figure out where Soko is DJing that night.

4 The best advice may be to stay in with tea and telly, but if the above sounds more likely, then congratulations young lady 'cause – just like Sheila – you're a punk rocker. Like a drunk packing for the airport, throw all your worldly possessions in an old battle-scarred bag (i.e., your black tote bag crammed with a plethora of nonessential items you insist you can't leave the house without). Or, the polar opposite, a clutch so small you can't even fit your phone in it. Aesthetically, either will look dope.

5 When it comes to choosing shoes, don't overthink it. My advice is to wear flats; it's way better to be comfortable than to break an ankle (I speak from experience: apparently, my Achilles' heel is my Achilles' heel). A pair of old Dr. Martens, your fave ballerina flats, or if you're feeling rowdy, a pair of colourful Converse. Anything you can both dance and run in.

PRO TIP

My main advice on **accessorising this look:**
- **More is more.** Pile on your silver jewellery, rings and bracelets.
- **Be creative.** Wear safety pins as earrings and chip your nail varnish on the subway into town.
- **Counterpoint the punk babe energy** with a drop of Chanel No. 5. Those who recognise it will be intrigued to find it wafting from such a hot mess.

Talent, they say, borrows, but genius steals.

Tweed Perfection

OK, I get it: Gabrielle Chanel was wooed by a charming, elegant Englishman. We've all been there: sucked in by that classic old world sophistication, infused with that subtle blend of charm and arrogance. This particular chap introduced Coco to the English countryside and all its marvellous quirks. Which of course included an integral part of her fellow's wardrobe: tweed. Famous as she already was for helping herself to elements of menswear and repurposing them for women, here she similarly appropriated the traditionally British fabric, establishing it as a key element of her quintessentially Parisian label. Talent, they say, borrows, but genius steals. I can relate to this practice, more than once having found myself on tour with no clean laundry and dipping into the boys' suitcases.

Tweed is a coarse woollen fabric. Traditionally used for Scottish and Irish outdoor attire, it was also used for sportswear as it's moisture resistant and durable. Yet after convincing her tea-drinking beau to commission a Scottish factory to produce her tweed fabrics in the 1930s, Coco's innate ingenuity and creativity soon found her weaving different materials in with the wool – including silk, cotton and even cellophane. In 1957, Coco first presented the now famous 'Chanel tweed' in the shape of a small jacket with golden buttons, a classic and oft-referenced piece in the Chanel canon. A useful way to illustrate how Chanel tweed compares to traditional tweed would be to wheel out the old, lazy (but fun) French vs British comparisons: Chanel tweed is more subtle, vibrant, less practical (one shouldn't assume that Chanel tweed is thorn-proof), it's a slice more snobby and while we're still awaiting our researcher's conclusive data, we have it on good authority that wearers of Chanel tweed are better kissers.

While it remained a staple of the Chanel house for decades, the arrival of Karl Lagerfeld at the company in 1983 heralded a modern reworking of tweed. Innovative as he was, he soon began challenging Chanel's more conservative aesthetic, making small adjustments to

From the Chanel S/S 2007 RTW collection press kit, photographed by Karl Lagerfeld.

iconic pieces while maintaining their recognisable integrity. Karl was clever. These changes happened gradually and so, by degrees, he began taking the brand into the twenty-first century.

At the beginning of the 1990s his innovative designs proved ground breaking: introducing denim to the brand and weaving tweed with neon wool, thus bringing a punk feel to Chanel. It was a quiet revolution for the brand, now spearheading an 'intellectual sexiness' – one that made it accessible to a hip, younger clientele. In my view, the stroke of genius was combining denim (beloved of rebellious youth) with tweed (loved by the upper classes). Karl understood that despite being innately culturally disparate, both materials have a raw, dry finish which makes them work well together.

The stroke of genius was combining denim with tweed.

Tweed Jacket with Denim

Make It Your Own

Nowadays there's an established harmony in the joyously mismatched discord of these two materials. Head to toe in full tweed looks overbearing; unless you're a farmer corralling sheep in the wild Scottish Highlands, you may find yourself raising eyebrows, not to mention your body temperature.

The same could be said for the head-to-toe denim look, affectionately known as the Canadian tuxedo, the perfect attire for all black-tie lumberjack events, including formal maple syrup tastings and polar bear weddings.

But combining the two in an ensemble can create magic:

1 Mix a **tweed jacket with a humble pair of jeans** for the quintessential *passe-partout* outfit – wearable anywhere from work to cocktails with friends to bailing your boyfriend out of jail. My favourite way to sport this look is with a **metal T-shirt**, a bunch of **gold jewellery** and a pair of bashed-up **Converse**.

2 Dress it up by wearing **high-waisted jeans, a delicate belt and a classic white T-shirt**. Knock this look out of the park by adding a pair of **knee-high heeled boots**.

Facing page: Tweed jacket paired with ripped jeans from my fashion line.

Pages 112–13: Finale of the Chanel F/W 2007–8 RTW show (background); Chanel runway photos and backstage snapshots from 2004–8.

Marc Jacobs, in his SoHo studio, by Stephen Mark Sullivan.

MARC JACOBS

Style is a Lifestyle

Style is knowing who you are,
what you want to say, and not giving a damn.

Attributed to Gore Vidal

If you break down Marc's personal style, you'll find his artistic and musical influences hiding in plain view.

EVEN THOUGH MARC JACOBS IS A CHAMELEON who wears his heart on his sleeve, he has always remained his defiantly idiosyncratic self.

How does one's inner soul affect one's art? As questions for the ages go, this one is a deep cut. I guess the answer would be that one's art can change drastically somewhere in between one's freedom of expression and one's personal struggles.

Heralded as a prodigy at the start of his career, Marc then remained an omnipresent force in the fashion world for the next thirty years, ever challenging the conventional ways to approach style. Everything to do with his creative process exudes nonchalance, and the results, while achingly contemporary, always betray a nostalgic affection for the arts. If you break down Marc's personal style, you'll find his artistic and musical influences hiding in plain view.

He's a spontaneous, mythical creature, wise beyond his years. His attention to detail has always led me to suspect he's possessed of a photographic memory. As Johnny Rotten says, 'he don't miss a trick, love'.

Sadly, over the years this business has a habit of hardening the arteries. Marc still has an undeniable twinkle flickering in his eyes, however, one of the things I love the most about him is his courageous spirit. Plus, he's actually interested in things outside of fashion (what blasphemy is this?!?).

I have been a fan of his for years, since the early 1990s when I was a scruffy duckling in Canada and grunge popped by to save us all from that 1980s fashion wave and those frightful perms. Who could forget his work with Sonic Youth on their 'Sugar Kane' video? A brutal satire on the nature of catwalk fashion culture that had all models (male and female) with more than two brain cells wishing they were Kim Gordon. That whole Perry Ellis show made my little prepubescent head spin like that girl from *The Exorcist*. It's a testament to Marc's skill that grunge became a fashion staple rather than a fad – embraced universally by all shapes and sizes in all seasons. Fashion moves in a cyclical manner (my excuse for never throwing clothes away). Everything will have its moment but rarely will it be seen as universally as this: looking like Thurston Moore circa 1992 never quite went out of style, did it? Grunge, the bastard child of 1960s garage and 1970s punk, revived the original, gritty spirit of rock 'n' roll.

With Marc at the S/S 2007 RTW show at the Armory in NYC, 11 September 2006.

A NEW YORK MINUTE

A Marc Jacobs show is a theatrical spectacle. Imagine Wednesday Addams taking a tumble down Alice in Wonderland's rabbit hole and coming out the other side to shake things up in time for tea (par-tea that is), the mood imbued with her timeless Goth/Victorian spirit.

You never forget your first Marc Jacobs show. The electricity in the air is palpable; you feel like you're part of something special, exciting and wickedly strange, even for a show in NYC. For us models, it felt like our season officially kicked off with Marc in the Big Apple. A sense compounded by the fact that by the time you got to London or Milan the first question a casting director would ask your respective agent was, invariably, 'Did she do Marc Jacobs?'.

In February 2006, a very pregnant Karen Elson opened the show and I was terrified as I walked right behind her that her waters would break on the catwalk! I had the honour of closing the show — my first for Marc — but found myself fighting off sleep during the preparatory fittings while his teams rallied around my exhausted frame, hemming and hawing (pun intended) about what I was to wear. Let me tell you: there ain't no fitting like a Marc Jacobs fitting. His shows are known for their elaborate styling that often emphasises layering; skirts worn over pants, leg warmers as gloves, bandanas as scarves, oversized grunge sweaters matched with puffy pants. This particular season my old friend flannel even made a comeback in the form of a wicked dress. Ever the inventive sartorial chef, Marc served a sparkling gold beret as the gloriously counterintuitive plat de résistance.

There's something for everyone in his eclectic style. In a Jacobs outfit, you're ready for any eventuality that life may throw at you. Should you need to leave the country suddenly, for example, you can wear your whole wardrobe and skip the suitcase. You just have to plan ahead for pit stops; getting undressed might take a minute.

I had my parents in tow that season in NYC, ostensibly to keep an eye on me. As such, I found myself embattled by both the Fun Police and the Fashion Police. There were, I was warned with stern disapprobation, to be no monkeyshines, no tomfoolery, not so much as the merest hint of malarkey. Saying that, my Pops soon became distracted by the very serious business of overseeing the NFL playoffs in the car with my adorable but opinionated driver. My indomitable and formidable mum bravely decided she'd come to all my shows and fittings. All thirty-eight of them. The poor wee thing was exhausted after two days, trying to keep up with our insane schedule, all the while running around trying to feed the girls backstage. By the time we got to my Marc fitting she was exhausted and fell asleep on a wooden chair in the middle of the frenzy. When Marc, patrolling the studios (orchestrating the chaos in his kindly idiosyncratic manner), found her, he quietly insisted and led her to his office, where he offered her his sofa for some shut eye, and even tucked her in! A bona fide sweetheart. Even in the eye of a storm — like the final preparations for a huge show, where the stress levels would have most of us mere mortals melting down — his calm leadership and innate humanity shine through.

Top right: Casting head shot.
Centre: Marc at the S/S 2007 RTW show in NYC, 11 September 2006.
Bottom: On the catwalk for the S/S 2013 RTW show in NYC, 10 September 2012.

oh babe I'll let you be you

I cant give you the mornin sun
if you dont it Now you better run
I cant let you apologize when it's them
out oh babe I can let you be now

But the FLOWER
of SAN FRANAND

the
FLOWERS of

How Long ho
have

A tall
rose

pav 4 N
doubl

car p
An

his way
his
the Mansion
(when)
memorizin
self
it
without farther
put
oceded
strike out
for the
again manhole
riend myself
u the doors

e doom
se find again

An Once again by friend
we meet on the End
thru the doors room's
An As you can
there's no one left in the wo

GRACE IN TOKYO

A few months later, Marc held a Louis Vuitton show in Tokyo, one of the most fascinating and bizarre cities in the world. I've spent a considerable amount of time in Japan throughout my career and I love everything about it. Exploring Tokyo is akin to visiting a metropolis on another planet. It's simultaneously crowded, yet strangely quiet, populated by exceedingly lovely and polite folk, whose deferential bonhomie is surpassed only by their affinity for creating and adhering to social rules and conventions. I could write volumes around my fascination with their myriad subcultures, meticulous attention to hairstyles, the food, the rich history.

Marc's Louis Vuitton show was staged in Yumenoshima Park in a custom-built marquee, with a dizzying gold decor. This Japan-based Jacobs jamboree coincided, to my quiet delight, with my birthday. If the chance to work with one of my favourite designers in one of my favourite cities wasn't enough to get my heart pounding, I was told that none other than her majesty Grace Jones was to perform at the after-party! I'm a lifelong rabid fan of this peerless force of nature, and my little brain was in a perpetual state of explosion during the weeks preceding the show.

Most of the girls flew together from NYC on the same plane — but as soon as the flight departed my excitement got the better of me and I'm told that I passed out, snoring quietly to myself the whole eighteen hours there. Apparently I missed quite the party (that's a first!). At least I was well rested for the show. Speaking of which — as well as it went and as impressive as it was — please indulge a fangirl and allow me to skip straight to Ms Jones's genius performance. It was a tempting daydream — like projecting oneself forward and backward in history — and it left all of us renewed with a tremendous zest for life in all its variety. Like being blessed by a Patti Smith or Nick Cave performance. Perhaps that's to be expected from such a transformative and unique artist; still, it knocks your heart for six.

I've been obsessed with Grace since the first time I heard 'Art Groupie' in my teens; her (now signature) reggae-inflected new wave tickled my fancy and haunted my dreams. Her voice, her charisma, was the essence of sex. Enough to awaken curiosity in the soul of any poor ambivalent teen. A feminist icon and contradictory force of nature, she's famously known for her explosive temper and her complicated love affairs; Grace Jones's fierce love life makes Joan Collins's sound like a cereal advert. She is the pure embodiment of everything that's punk, raw and glam rock in all its androgynous splendour. Her approach to life chimes profoundly with Marc's aesthetic; the sense of commonality and celebration that resonated still makes me emotional in retrospect.

Arriving at the venue wearing a purple velvet cape like the coolest Amazonian queen to walk the face of the earth, she started the performance with 'La Vie en Rose' (boom), followed by 'Nightclubbing' (double boom). Way to make an entrance! Transfixed and mesmerised, I danced off my little groupie bum, giving it everything I had with all my staple moves: the Shopping Cart, the Washing Machine, even the Running Man.

Top left and right: Walking the runway at the S/S 2007 RTW show in NYC, 11 September 2006.
Bottom right: Walking the F/W 2006-7 RTW show in NYC, 6 February 2006.

I ONCE READ THE BOOK
AND IT'S WORDS WERE
PURE & SIMPLE  
THE CITY WAS FLOOD
DESPAIR OF IT'S

THE MARKS
& SILENCE HAS REMOVED
DESTINY WALK THROUGH THE GARDEN
WAS YOUNG,
I HAD NO DOUBT.
I WAS MAS FOOLISH
AS the

you took your
Holy day
had i not been
that way
It was not mine
to take
you took your
heart away
it was not mine
to say
it was a holiday

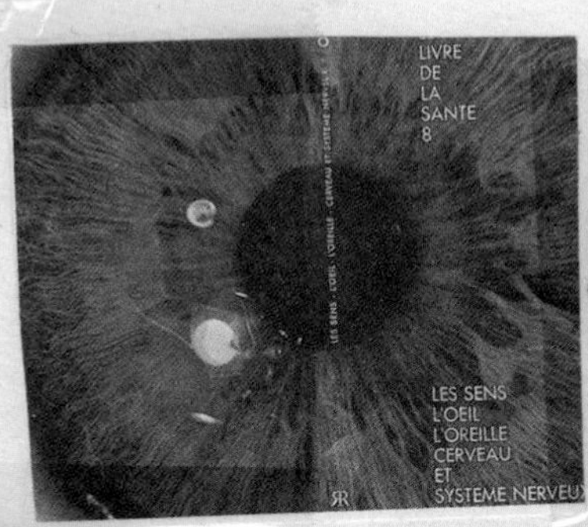

LIVRE
DE
LA
SANTE
8

LES SENS
L'OEIL
L'OREILLE
CERVEAU
ET
SYSTEME NERVEUX
SR

...

Grace Jones's fierce love life makes Joan Collins's sound like a cereal advert.

As I bumbled about after the gig, elated and sipping a flute of champagne, I spotted her with Marc at their table. I cautiously approached, trying to get closer to drink her in, all the while endeavouring to play it cool and not drool. Soon I was beckoned to join them. When Marc subtly mentioned it was my birthday, she turned and looked straight into my eyes, like a wild cat hypnotising its prey before pouncing. What followed left me so amazed you could have knocked me down with a feather. With a sound that seemed to rise from the very earth, she started singing 'Happy Birthday' in her signature deadpan purr. As Dame Jones finished her performance to one, overwhelmed and admittedly a little drunk, I started crying tears of Dom Perignon. Marc gave me a wink and a smile; he knew what he was doing. He made my year with that gesture, and I love him for it, just as I'll always love him for looking after my precious little mumma when I couldn't. What then ensued at the party following this seismic life event I'm afraid is very much a blur. Kudos to my friends for getting me on our flight back; I applaud you, whoever you are. Thanks to the mechanics of long-haul travel and how time zones behave, by the time we touched the tarmac at JFK it was my birthday again! But that, my friends, is another story.

Top: Grace Jones performing at the Louis Vuitton F/W 2006–7 after-party in Tokyo.
Bottom: An exterior shot of the venue in Tokyo, 7 June 2006.

le Catapillar

save me anyway

album:
Lust of the libertines
Is really quite tame

Well fame's such a sinister game
Oh I know
The taste of goulash in your mouth as you stumble of stage
Forget-me-nots bloom on this day then
But they wither with age

Oh I can deal with all the blood on my shoes
And the holes in my soul
My spirit is tainted all my tears are fainted
Just as long as you
You don't forget to
Uh-oh-oh
Cut me on the wall
By the graffiti of all the thing I just couldn't say
Shove me up the wall

Glam Rock Spirit

I've already bollocked on about how, when I was a thirteen-year-old Canadian Greebo, Marc Jacobs first came to my bug-eyed attention via Sonic Youth's video for their art-rock masterpiece 'Sugar Kane' (I urge anyone who has not yet seen it to plop this book down for five minutes and find it on YouTube, it's a belter), but as much as he did to cement 1990s thrift-shop stoner chic as a timeless fashion staple, his collections are as eclectic as his style and move organically through the seams of time, depending on the resonance of any particular story he wants to project through his work. Ultimately his collections are a melting pot of several cultural movements or different fashion periods; the 1960s pop generation is a predominant reference in his cuts but always with a spicy kick and an interesting plot twist. Expect the unexpected from Marc Jacobs: a touch of metallic, a sparkle of sequins, a wink to the sartorial order of glam rock – a musical subgenre that has, over the years, influenced some of his collections.

Exploding into the global zeitgeist in the 1970s, glam rock was as much about what you wore as what you listened to. It was sleazy, but seductive. Dirty, but debonair. Immoral, but immaculate. By the 1970s, the wave of the 1960s sexual revolution began to lose momentum globally and, as it ebbed, it revealed on the shore a new generation of kids who damn well weren't about to be embarrassed about their exuberance, no matter what their parents said. These brave, beautiful weirdos found their identity in the burgeoning new glam rock subculture, spearheaded by artists such as David Bowie, Roxy Music and T-Rex. Unlike today (in the West at least) where we can pretty much wear what we like without fear of becoming social pariahs, in the 1970s it took balls to proudly sport the kind of clothes synonymous with this music, and often resulted in black eyes. While this may have saved money on mascara, adhering to the aesthetic undeniably took a degree of steely integrity.

To incorporate Marc's eclectic style in the '20s (i.e., the 2020s), subtlety is the rule of thumb. Whereas you can go all out with grunge – Converse, ripped 501s, plaid shirt and a beanie, for example – a deft touch is in order to maximise the efficacy of the Glam MJ look (day to day that is; if you're heading out to a themed club night then by all means feel free to 'put a hat on a hat'). With that in mind, let's identify the main pieces in the genre's arsenal and how to have fun with them. These are big guns after all, and the aim is to catch the eye, not terrify.

Glam rock vibes by Philip Gay from an editorial for *Zoo Magazine* issue no. 19, 2008.

In my element in a
squat in Copenhagen.

Glam Rock Around the Clock

- **Commuting to work?** Find a cute **silk shirt** and calm it down
  with a **tank top**. If the shirt is paisley, keep the tank top muted. If
  the tank top is zigzag, choose a monotone silk shirt. Combine this
  with **high-waisted trousers**. Try not to choose a pair that is wildly
  higher than what you're used to, as the shift can make one a tad
  self-conscious.
- **Post-work drinks?** If we look at the 1970s redux designs by
  Jacobs (as well as Yves Saint Laurent, Pucci, Miu Miu and Tom
  Ford) over the last few years, **halter necks, platforms and
  Oxford bags** abound. Choose one or two of these elements as
  opposed to all of them. Weave them into your existing personal
  style, and find pieces that you feel comfortable in.
- **Going to a club** in Manhattan where they play Fischerspooner
  remixes and serve Harvey Wallbangers? Then you can get really
  creative. If you're planning to dance for hours, try a **1940s-esque
  sprig-print frock**. Adjust the hemline to taste (especially if you
  want to show off a pair of shoes). If your evening's plan is more
  propping up the bar and flirting loudly over the music with that
  boy you fancy, why not boldly try on a **three-piece trouser suit**
  for size? Glam rock was about androgyny, after all, and that goes
  both ways. If this feels a bit much, I often opt for a **tailored blazer
  with the sleeves rolled up** (it's OK, post-1980s rolled-up jacket
  sleeves are ironic and cool again).

PRO TIP

Add some **subtly glittered
makeup,** colour coordinated with
your clothes. How heavily or
discreetly you apply it depends
on the occasion, or your mood
(god knows the latter dictates my
makeup choices).

Right and pages 128
and 129: Portraits by
Venetia Scott for an
i-D magazine special
issue on Marc Jacobs,
in Hyde Park, London,
summer 2006.

Layer Up

The spirit of Marc Jacobs' layering style is by
its very nature loud, Technicolour, and exciting.
It's a thrilling and culturally rich world to enjoy,
but its irrepressible nature means it can be
easy to overdo. This word of caution by no
means is to say it's something to be afraid of
however – we can find and lend freedom to
our inner alter egos by diving into his universe.
While you're getting ready to go out, find a
full-length mirror and whack on 'All the Young
Dudes' by Mott the Hoople (or David Bowie's
brilliant cover). If you look good while that tune
is blaring, then you've nailed it.

`PRO TIP`

Marc Jacobs Accessories

- First, let me be clear, I've learned from personal
  experience that **there's nothing you can't do or face
  in a pair of Marc Jacobs glasses;** I'm pretty sure that
  empires were conquered in them.
- And second, **there's nothing you can't fit into a Marc
  Jacobs bag,** including my ex-boyfriend's ego. Believe
  me that it is a spacious accessory; to this day it's my
  official go-bag in case my cover is blown and I have
  to leave the country and relocate in search of a new
  identity.

Nicolas Ghesquière by Nicolas Guerin
for *Self Assignment*, Paris, 18 June 2006.

NICOLAS GHESQUIÈRE

Master Tailor

Never forget that what is timeless today
was once new.

Nicolas Ghesquière

A great garment always starts with the cut.

THE TIME HAS COME FOR A SERIOUS FRENCH
LESSON. Or rather, I should say, a lesson in serious
Frenchness.

To describe Nicolas Ghesquière and his work in
a pithy, succinct way is plain impossible. Any attempt
to put this man into words should by rights end up sounding like
surrealist prose, an accumulation of adjectives and superlatives worthy
of the great dialogues of New Wave films: rigorous, cerebral, loyal,
impatient, intellectual, precise, architectural, Parisian, futuristic, athletic,
neoclassical, visionary, ethnic but urban, hybrid and graphic, volumetric,
daring, rigorous, geometric, perfectionist, subtle, explorer, powerful and
elegant. And that's just his hair!

If I absolutely had to sum him up in a concise phrase, I'd go with
an oft-used expression that happens to be entirely suitable: crème
de la crème. This turn of phrase also happens to be one that neatly
characterises his first collections at Balenciaga. To my good fortune
this was also the time I was accepted into the intimacy of his studio.
Nicolas's outstanding team included Marie-Amélie, Florent, Bouchra,
Julien and many other gifted souls. I was blessed to witness one of
those rare creative moments where a designer has cemented his
position as head of a house, embracing its codes to perfection and
pushing its creations past expectation.

When I was part of the catwalk team for Spring/Summer 2008 (a
collection that has since become cult) I had yet to become fully aware
of my privilege to participate in a key moment in fashion history. These
volumes from another dimension, the noble but technical materials,
the strength of the all-over prints and the razor-sharp architecture of
the silhouettes were a complete break from the codes and norms of
the time. It was, of course, daring. But as Nicolas relayed in *Madame
Figaro*, 'what is timeless today was once new'.

On the runway
at Balenciaga
F/W 2006–7 RTW.

GEOMETRY AT WORK

I started working with Nicolas in the early 2000s as a newcomer to Paris when I took the gig as the official fitting model for Balenciaga. I welcomed the opportunity to get an inside look at the creative process. Those were halcyon days, spent working with and observing a small yet incredibly talented team who oversaw every creation's minute detail in the studio.

I witnessed how an idea or a simple inspiration was meticulously researched and transformed from sketch to garment. Most of the time these pieces were constructed fragment by fragment on my body (that's right, a fitting model is a live mannequin): from a fragment of material to a sculpted, futuristic, geometric shape.

This process required serious commitment from the entire team, long hours that stretched into the early mornings. It was during these magical twilight moments ('when the light in the sky makes it difficult to distinguish between dog and wolf', as Nicolas would say) that Mr Ghesquière, like many great artists, did his best work.

The days leading up to shows were always a whirlwind of emotions and organised chaos. Oftentimes I'd end up sleeping standing up (a useful trick to master in my line of work), even stealing the odd power nap under Nicolas's desk! I didn't mind the long hours though, as I felt very much at home in the Rue de Sèvres studio.

Interesting conversations always echoed in the halls in that creative cauldron of a workspace. Funny anecdotes were shared during smoke breaks or over the alarming amount of coffee brewed in the small but serviceable kitchen located in a narrow corridor at the end of the studio, which was always replete with a seemingly never-ending supply of macarons. The kitchen was everyone's favourite place to be; we'd cram in there like sardines every chance we got

(on reflection, it may have had something to do with the macarons).

Those were impressionable years; I was just a kid trying to figure out who I was and what I wanted in life. I learned so much from Nicolas: the importance of strength in one's conviction, the value of a strong work ethic, to never give up when life gets too hard, to never settle or compromise for mediocrity.

Nicolas is a colossally talented and magnetic force. The passion he has for his work is impossible not to admire. He's a visionary who's not afraid to roll up his sleeves; no detail is ever overlooked, no corner ever cut. He strives for perfection and won't stop until he achieves it. First and foremost a master tailor, he understands a great garment always starts with the cut. Those hours I spent standing statue-still, spellbound, watching the hypnotic dexterity of his sewing pins, remain crystal clear and magical in my memory. Like a sponge I silently soaked up as much knowledge as I could retain. For example, I learned how you make an 'epaulette cigarette', officially my favourite cigarette shoulder pad! I learned how you can sculpt, manipulate and modify a pattern to design a garment before it's made. But the master lesson I took away was the importance of always being cognisant of the interplay between a garment's geometry and form and the silhouette of the person wearing it.

It wasn't all graft; even a grand couturier like Nicolas can let his hair down. The time we spent rolling around on the grass with Freja at Andy Warhol's house in Montauk; the wonderful day we spent under the lens of Paolo Roversi with Françoise Hardy in Paris, these memories are mine to treasure as much as I cherish all he taught me. And I'm grateful in spades for the life lessons and opportunities he gifted me.

Clockwise from top left: Backstage with Nicolas at Balenciaga F/W RTW 2006–7; Balenciaga by Nicolas Ghesquière, S/S 2006 RTW campaign shot by David Sims; backstage portrait for my first Balenciaga show, 2005.

butterflies went out at noon
waltzed above a stream,
en stepped straight through the firmament
rested on a way

d then together bore
a shining
ough never

their coming

'T was so unlike the crumb
The birds and I had often shared
In Nature's dining-room.

The plenty hurt me, 't was so new,--
Myself felt ill and odd,
As berry of a mountain bush
Transplanted to the road.

Nor was I hungry; so I found
That hunger was a way
Of persons outside windows,
The entering takes away.

Tell him I only said the pronoun out.
And left the verb and the pronoun out.

Tell him just how the fingers hurried
Then how they waded, slow, slow, slow--
And then you wished you had eyes in your pages,
So you could see what moved them so.

"Tell him it wasn't a practised writer,
You guessed, from looking at the way the sentence toiled;
You could hear the bodice tug, behind you,
As if it held but the might of a child;
You almost pitied it, you, it worked so.
Tell him-- no, you may quibble there,
For it would split his heart to know it,
And then you and I were silenter.

"Tell him night finished before we finished,
And the old clock kept neighing 'day!'
And you got sleepy and begged to be ended--
What could it hinder so, to say?
Tell him just how she sealed you, cautious,
But if he ask where you are hid
Until to-morrow,--happy letter!
Gesture, coquette, and shake your head!

BALENCIAGA

It's All I have to bring to-day,
  This, and my heart beside,
This, and my heart, and all the fields,
  And all the meadows wide.
Be sure you count, should I forget, --
  Some one the sum could tell, --
This, and my heart, and all the bees
  Which in the clover dwell.

Fashion Fundamentals

Curate Your Look

The Ghesquière look is refined and complex, 'geek chic' ('*intello-chic*' in French). Every detail, every shape and texture is meticulously studied, along with their broader societal and cultural relevance. The end result is an impressive accomplishment of harmonious synergy.

Over the years Nicolas has made a life's work of demonstrating to us mere mortals how the correct marriage of a garment's architecture to one's silhouette is fundamental. It's about **creating a harmony of lines and curves, a dialogue of volumes and colours**.

Before starting, the ballet dancer in me invites you to **consider your body's posture**. I know it sounds obvious, but we've all been guilty of buying clothes we love for one reason or another that just don't suit us. And believe me, there are plenty of clothes I love that just look weird on a ballet dancer! I find this simple routine before trying pieces on helps me know if it's right for me, for my frame; you may wanna try it yourself:

Find a mirror. Raising your head and standing up straight, relax your shoulders, gently drawing them back and down. Raise your hands above your head then let them fall by your sides. Then relax and slowly shake any tension left in you out. If there's room, take a little stroll to remind yourself how you look as you walk. This awareness of your body will help you **make the right choice of shapes and cut**, choices that bring balance to the silhouette, clever choices to enhance your strengths and catch the eye.

I'm not making headlines to reiterate here that our appearance carries a certain currency, especially on first impressions. Even before we've exchanged words our reptilian brain judges within seconds (twenty, on average), subconsciously and instinctively. As daft as it is, this initial nonverbal communication tends to linger, so we're doing ourselves a favour when we manage with subtlety and efficiency the message we want to project to the world. We can have fun with it too. Whichever role you want to play – from the energy of a businesswoman to the languid sartorial poetry of an artist to the deft provocation of a seductress – it pays dividends to choose the right elements to serve your goals.

On the catwalk
for Balenciaga
F/W 2007–8 RTW.

Consider the volumes (narrow or exuberant, sharp or voluptuous), the colours (sober or indecent, elegant or disruptive) and the many adjustment variables. There are endless combinations possible to finesse what you wish to communicate. As you build this vocabulary, you'll add more strings to your bow, empowering yourself to move through the world with your best foot forward.

Put simply, we need to think before we dress. Working with Nicolas taught me that the more you intellectualise your relationship with clothing, the more fun you can have. That being said, nurturing one's instinct and talent for improvisation is equally crucial. Both are key. Prioritise what you buy: you gotta build a solid toolbox before embarking on DIY operations.

I can't overstate the importance of acquiring the right versatile pieces that combine easily with each other. Let's face it, we don't all have walk-in Narnia-esque wardrobes, sadly. The aim is to build an efficient arsenal of killer clothing options, not a Tetris wall of sequinned tops.

This process will be much easier (and fun) if you create a mood board to get the ball rolling. If wall space is at a premium, build a Pinterest inspiration board with visual references to the themes close to your heart. I love using an old-fashioned cork board and pinning magazine cut-outs; I couldn't tell you how many images of 1930s women I've accumulated over the years!

How you carry yourself in each outfit is paramount too, looping back to the importance of good posture. Throw yourself into the persona, the role of each ensemble. Personally, I'm guilty of absorbing ideas from the silver screen, and I encourage you to have fun doing the same. Study the slightest movements of your favourite heroines, memorising the innocuous little gestures that'll bring your figure to life. The way you hold a cigarette, brush a strand of hair from your brow and so on. Soon enough your fluency with how to dress and hold yourself for each occasion will require less and less effort, eventually becoming second nature. Your intuition will draw you artfully and instinctively to the right pieces when you open your wardrobe in the morning, and the poise and confidence this will afford you will clear the path for you to get to where you're going. Of course clothes aren't everything. But at their best they can be a part of who you are, what you want people to see in you. And that's creative, empowering and fun.

Facing page: Balenciaga S/S 2006 RTW; and a friend's illustration.

Above: Backstage snap at the Balenciaga S/S 2007 RTW show, by Robert Fairer.

Pages 140–41: Balenciaga by Nicolas Ghesquière, S/S 2006 RTW campaign shot by David Sims.

BALENCIAGA

And so it begins:
Our dream of a future where the world embraces equality
and love.
Where a shared vision of peace resonates across the
frontiers of ignorance.
Where courage and truth speak louder than hate.
Like the winds of change, love is a force to be reckoned
with.
Placed in the hands of fate, it's not limited by age,
gender or race.
It's invisible sometimes, yet present all over the place.
Somehow many springs have come and gone.
Where we've turned moments into memories,
And memories into history.
To seek a new beginning,
Where equality and the freedom to love
Are rights given to all.
This fuel that makes change a reality will not be lost
in a quiet cage.
This right to love
Is as vital as the right to breathe,
As is the right to express one's own true identity,
Which allows every soul to live peacefully in truth.

My own poem on an engraving by Léon Benett from Jules Verne's *Robur the Conqueror*, 1886.

THE GAME CHANGERS

Edward Enninful
Inez & Vinoodh

Change will not come if we wait
for some other person or if we wait
for some other time. We are the ones we've been
waiting for. We are the change that we seek.

Barack Obama

Edward Enninful

The Visionary

The conscientious tide is turning … and Edward is leading the charge.

AN EMINENTLY QUOTABLE, INNOVATIVE AND ALWAYS FASCINATING ENGLISH LAD, Edward's imagination and keen eye propelled the pages of *i-D* magazine and more recently the chronicles of British *Vogue* into the future. Edward is a freethinker, always on the hunt for an inspiring story line, and in the process of doing so he tends to behave more like an activist than an editor.

I first met him at my debut modelling job in New York: a Mulberry campaign that was photographed by the great Steven Meisel and styled by Edward. I remember it like it was yesterday. As my cab stopped in front of Pier 59 studio on West Side Highway, I paused to take a deep breath and gather my faculties before entering. As it happened I didn't allow myself too long, as Cheri's warning that she would 'literally kill me' if I was even one minute late was still ringing in my ears. For a young model this was a very important shoot, and I was green and nervous. But when I walked in, Edward quickly put me at ease with his warmth, kindness and the familiarity of his affable British brogue.

I must admit I was starstruck when I met him; as a teenager I would run to the newsstand monthly and devour *i-D* magazine cover to cover, as, like for all London school kids, grunge had become my religion.

I could always recognise an Edward story in *i-D*, where he was the youngest ever fashion director for a major international publication. Being a youngster himself, he knew what the kids wanted to read and see, creating something sexy, provocative and grungy with a pinch of British chic – something he looked for in his subjects and drew out of them in their attitude.

And yes, I say subjects, because Edward is undeniably the driving avant-garde force of the British Fashion Royal Family (BFRF). To labour a metaphor, we could look at the fashion industry as being formed of various powerful 'families', and each has particular and idiosyncratic qualities: the Parisians, meticulous and fastidiously French. The Italians, outlandish and passionate. The innovative American squad. Then there are the British. A curious bunch, as – despite undeniably keeping a foot in the past – since the sexual revolution of the 1960s and the punk explosion in the late 1970s, they've led the charge when it comes to embracing change. Cool Britannia's modern fashion aristocratic lineage

Edward Enninful
with his dog Ru,
by Emma Summerton.

Photo by Craig
McDean for British
Vogue, May 2018.

From left:
*VITTORIA CERETTI
HALIMA ADEN
ADUT AKECH
FARETTA RADIC
PALOMA ELSESSER
RADHIKA NAIR
YOON YOUNG BAE
FRAN SUMMERS
SELENA FORREST*

includes Alexander McQueen, Vivienne Westwood, Anna Wintour, Grace Coddington, Katie Grand, Venetia Scott, Craig McDean, Katy England, Lady Amanda Harlech, David Bailey, Tim Walker, Suzy Menkes and Pat McGrath.

The BFRF – or, as the French call them, the British mafia – knew how to pass the crown to a new generation by acquiring a new monarch in Edward Enninful. Throughout his impeccable career he continued to blaze a progressive trail, holding the position of contributing fashion editor at both American and Italian *Vogue* and creative fashion director at *W* magazine, until accepting his current role at British *Vogue* in 2017. His achievements were recognised by another monarch in 2016, when Queen Elizabeth II bestowed on him an Order of the British Empire (OBE).

Edward has brilliantly modernised British *Vogue*, earning tremendous respect and admiration for his unflinching efforts to bring more inclusivity and diversity to the fashion industry. This he has done without eschewing Britain's proud fashion heritage, regularly featuring perennial BFRF crown jewels such as Kate Moss, Naomi Campbell, the late Stella Tennant, Karen Elson, Twiggy or Erin O'Connor.

Behind the scenes he's been a positive force too, shaping the future landscape by recognising and supporting a new generation of photographers and models. As conscientious as he is kind, he will forever have my love and admiration for being such a vocal advocate for the importance of sustainability in clothing production. It is a passion he shares with Prince Charles, as they discussed together in an interview for British *Vogue* that spanned from HRH's timeless style to ecologically responsible fashion. On a personal level, I'm forever grateful for the way he adroitly helped shape my own career, as he did for others, leading by example. In a broader context, his human and mature voice rises above the chaotic world of fashion, and we're all glad he's there.

His résumé is impressive! I consider myself incredibly lucky to have got to know him simply as Edward (before the OBE): a sensible soul who always had a kind word for everyone around. The best place to start if one has plans to change the world.

I look at fashion today and see a more diverse, inclusive industry, where issues of abuse are brought to light and addressed, not swept away. Where positive body image is beginning to be celebrated. There's still a long way to go. But times are changing. The conscientious tide is turning, and with it the passionate flair of the rebel cavalry is awakening all around us, and Edward is leading the charge.

Inez & Vinoodh

THE FIRST TIME I WORKED WITH INEZ & VINOODH, I realised quickly they're in a league of their own. A dynamic Dutch duo, they've spent a lifetime refining the art of their imagery. Recognised as giants in their field, they operate as a team in harmonious tandem and synchronicity. When faced with one of their powerful photographs, it becomes evident they're not chasing perfection, but truth.

I remember our first shoot together in vivid detail: I stood quietly in the soft light that illuminated the studio from a stained glass window. I remember feeling that the atmosphere it created was more of an ethereal glow from long ago than rays of light, which fell on Inez and then on me and everything in between.

By and by, Inez filtered in, and with mesmerising grace began deftly rearranging the set like a 3D puzzle.

Holding her hands up like Marcel Marceau and closing one eye, she moved her forearms in a slow arc, thumbs and index fingers outlining a rectangle, until I too swung into her frame. A slight smile flickered across her face when she saw my wide eyes blinking at her in transfixed awe.

The speed with which I saw her observe the room's contents (me included) and know exactly what the end result would be was remarkable. Within minutes she saw how the photographs would look. Like a sculptor who contemplates a raw block of marble and sees the statue before hammering the first chisel, she effortlessly saw the room, the light, the props, and within a minute foresaw what she could create with these raw materials. Like a painter, she was transforming a blank canvas into a photograph.

There are countless unforgettable moments that come to mind when remembering the times we worked together: the epic *Self Service* cover story, the various *V* magazine editorials or our *Vanity Fair* special with Sean Lennon. What's truly amazing about working with these two is their formidable gift as storytellers. They give you a narrative that makes you feel like you're a part of the creative process, rather than just a mannequin or a prop. They give you the freedom to explore a world of possibilities with body language and facial expressions, to use your imagination to examine different sides of the human condition while portraying a

Above: Inez van Lamsweerde and Vinoodh Matadin in a personal photograph.

character. Personally, this makes me more inclined to participate fully and give it my best, leading me to ask myself questions about my character like 'Who is she now? How does she feel?'. No doubt this is part of why they've remained the sweethearts of the fashion industry for the past thirty-five years, while maintaining their artistic edge and integrity.

It's a hackneyed cliché, isn't it, that some 'world-famous fashion photographers have enormous egos'? And a flair for the dramatic arts. Inez & Vinoodh, however, are on the other side of the scale – always composed, calm and kind. They never needed theatrics because they simply have talent.

SELF SERVICE

The concept for our *Self Service* editorial was this: two parallel universes that somehow collide in the same hotel suite at the St Regis in NYC. Two different women, representing the aesthetic of two different decades. The second model was my pal Hilary Rhoda, the quintessential American bombshell and utterly intimidating natural beauty. They transformed her into a fierce 1980s babe, along the lines of Brooke Shields or Joan Collins, both divas that defined a decade. She portrayed an OTT beautiful woman, confident in her role as a sex symbol. Her voluminous hair and multicoloured eye makeup were overshadowed only by an unflinching stare that made you wonder: is she plotting a military coup, or trying to remember if she'd left the iron on (but in a sexy, 'Helmut Newton babe leaves the iron on' kind of way)?

My character was a modern interpretation of Penelope Tree. As drawn by Tim Burton. With definite shades of the girl from *The Ring*. Inhabiting a 1960s avant-garde mentality, she was a combination of eccentricity and innocence, part iconic fringe, part Antonioni's *Blow-Up*. Agile and wild, she possessed enough kinetic energy to power Manhattan's electrical grid for a week. I hadn't jumped around like that since I had seen New Order in the 1990s in Manchester. My hair definitely developed a mind of its own and become as much a part of the story as the decor, inflicting anarchy in a bourgeois hotel. I guess 'hair rebellion' isn't always pretty but it can definitely be fun. Her personality was as much of a muddle as my own. A caricature of punk-ish havoc.

All of this happened under the watchful eye and precise direction of Suzanne Koller. Way more than a stylist, Suzanne is a true artistic director. Throughout her stellar career at *Self Service* (the magazine she cofounded with Ezra Petronio) and *Le Monde*,

she has consistently portrayed with aplomb a confident vision of femininity, creating timeless images that are at once modern, poetic, strong and sensual.

This particular *Self Service* shoot was emblematic of her work (devoted to her obsession with beige!) and, true to form, Suzanne's gamble here was audacious, as the story could have easily turned into a fiasco. I'm shorter than Hilary and our facial structures have nothing in common, but she found a way to utilise our differences to great effect, transforming the mood with a percussive energy that is evident in the images. Her styling was a true *je ne sais quoi* of peculiar accessories and glamorous gowns, and she had the unique task of separating the two universes by their idiosyncratic chronologies, all the while creating a beautiful cohesion. When the magic happens there's only one thing to do: watch and learn. That's exactly what I did that day.

There's always a surreal moment of calm and serenity as you stand on set, right before the clicking of camera shutters commences. The power of that liminal quiet always left an impression on me. It's usually the time I close my eyes and take a deep breath. That day, I remember feeling that we were about to create something very special. The dedication and attention to detail of the whole crew was inspiring.

I've always felt a little more at ease breathing through the endless imaginative possibilities while being directed by these two ever-trustworthy souls. The feeling of letting go, losing the anxiety of needing perfect control of my body (which so often has better ideas then my head in these moments) is a gift. No emotion was ever wasted with them: sometimes unanticipated mistakes produce unexpectedly perfect photographs.

Pages 151–55: On the cover and with Hilary Rhoda for the *Self Service* no. 24, S/S 2006,
photo shoot by Inez & Vinoodh, styled by Suzanne Koller.

self service

RE
BEGIN
NING

ISSUE N°24 SPRING/SUMMER 2006 15€

VANITY FAIR
FOR FASHION ROCKS

Probably one of my all-time favourite shoots, the *Vanity Fair* special for Fashion Rocks with my friend and collaborator Sean Lennon was a true fusion of the twin worlds of fashion and music. This epic shoot took place in the Hamptons, and our base camp was none other than Inez and Vinoodh's house. They used their superpower to freeze time and capture beautiful images and — like Snoop might say — crop 'em like they're hot. That day those two meant business, and quickly put us at ease with their confident yet playful direction, intuition and spontaneity. When well executed, photography presents a unique way of feeling, of touching, of loving. What is caught on film is captured forever, remembering those little things long after you have forgotten the details.

We started the day bombing about a sunny beach with wind and feathers in our hair; Sean looking roguish and movie-star handsome in a tuxedo, me in an anything but low-key top hat and chiffon dress. We joked how the premise should be improbable — sure, just a couple of friends inconspicuously strolling along the shore — but what's funny was this wasn't actually that odd of a scenario. We'd been spotted wearing far more outlandish outfits on a normal day walking to the supermarket.

The subsequent celluloid conceit found us tooling around the Hamptons in an achingly cool 1969 Volkswagen, blaring an old 8-track of The Doors. Not sure why, but my request to keep the car was met with nervous laughter! When I blinked seriously at them and started suggesting my people speak to their people about it, they stopped laughing and hurried us along to the next set, which found us entirely incapable of keeping a straight face, head to toe in suede Balenciaga and perched in a rickety wooden rowboat (admittedly, this scenario was unlikely, even for us).

Ostensibly, the purpose of this shoot was to announce that Sean and I would be presenters for the VH1 Fashion Awards to be held the following September. But the best laid plans of mice and men....

As things transpired, the following September we temporarily lost Sean to the Papua New Guinea jungle. We were terribly worried, as you may imagine, but it turns out we shouldn't have been, actually, because all he was doing was eschewing mundane activities such as presenting awards at ceremonies in favour of stumbling across and connecting with a native tribe. The tux on a beach doesn't seem so unusual, in perspective, does it?

Pages 157–59: With Sean Lennon in the Hamptons for a *Vanity Fair* September issue photo shoot by Inez & Vinoodh, August 2007.

Under the Influence
ROCK

Above: Captain's log: a page from my journal.

Page 160: I got this 1923 hand-beaded dress at an auction in New York.
I thought I was going to be married and buried in it ... hopefully not on the same day.

ENFANTS TERRIBLES

Babyshambles
Peter Doherty
Hedi Slimane

It was the best of times,
it was the worst of times.

From *A Tale of Two Cities* by Charles Dickens

The Shambles

We lived in the present, oblivious to consequences, blinded by the foolishness of youth.

WHILE BUBBLING AWAY IN THE MIND OF YOUNG PETER DOHERTY FOR YEARS, Babyshambles smudged their way onto the radar globally around 2003. Since then the sometimes lovable, sometimes infuriating band members have remained a permanent, if turbulent part of my life. At turns thorns in my side or unlikely saviours, for better or for worse I'll always consider them family.

On and off, I spent much of the mid-2000s in their company. These were dream-like careless days, with no second act in sight. We lived in the present, oblivious to consequences, blinded by the foolishness of youth while the future looked on, shaking its head, willing us to realise that we knew nothing of its work. My ever-faithful friend Sally and I call these 'the war years': an odd phase in my life where reality became stranger than fiction, the fallout of which still corrodes with a kind of psychedelic shell shock, and brings back a degree of post-traumatic stress.

Toast erratic stresses in eight dresses.

Appearances were always deceiving and no one was to be trusted, including ourselves; smoke 'n' mirrors was never just an illusion.

Every day was a new drama: some press scandal, a band member's arrest, a missed gig here, a band feud there, someone going MIA or losing their passport on the day they were supposed to travel.

When I attempt to recall episodes from this era, it can feel as if I fell asleep on the back of their tour bus as we departed London in 2003, then woke up as we rolled into Paris in 2008.

Trials and tribulations aside, the fact remains that they wrote a phenomenal number of beautifully imperfect songs, a body of work that strikes straight to the soul. Undeniably honest music and lyrics that embodied what they were going through at the time. Yes, their recordings (and certainly their shows) were peppered with false notes, mistakes and scrappiness, but around that time the industry was busy whitewashing guitar music with protocols and quantised, careerist ambitions. These boys plugged straight into their amps, remembering to tune their guitars if the crowd was lucky. How the songs sounded changed from day to day, from gig to gig. Not a formula for global domination, but refreshingly authentic. They sounded great, because they felt every note and believed every word; it's that realisation – how emotion and content are the most valuable assets an artist could hold – that makes them who they are.

They left their mark in music with relevance and honesty.

The lads on the *Shotter's Nation* tour, looking at the wrong camera, by Pennie Smith.

ON THE ROAD

It was my first time in Glasgow, the magnificent Scottish city and birthplace of our very own 'Sally Queen of Scots'. Between hitting the outskirts of the city and parking up at the venues, I became excited at the prospect of sightseeing and discovering the city, but even more enthusiastic to get off the tour bus after arguing with Peter for six hours straight. As we arrived at the Barrowland (which feels more like a gladiatorial arena then a venue), I couldn't help but be impressed by the raw punk energy of the kids queuing around the block — they were by far the most intimidating and stylish crowd I've ever seen. All sporting a no-nonsense, stripped down, 'f*ck you, Dad' look. Leather bomber jackets, ripped T-shirts and dirty jeans held together by a frayed thread of great expectations. After the gauntlet run to get inside (the artist entrance is conspiratorially placed beside the box office), we decided to remain indoors to explore this beautiful old venue.

By the time the gig was in full swing I watched, transfixed, as the crowd stomped their feet on the bouncing floors (the Barrowland has one of those old Northern soul sprung dance floors), echoing Shambles lyrics like war cries up to the rafters. It felt like the whole place was going to collapse, but not before those riot kids might break through the security barrier and destroy everything in their wake (after what happened at the Astoria a few years before, even the seasoned local security seemed a little on edge). Stage invasions have been a hallmark of Shambles shows from day one,

and this mob didn't seem too shy. As a venue, traditionally the Barrowland ain't for the faint of heart. If the kids don't like a set, they let the band know. I think it's that 'no bullsh*t' spirit that makes them love Babyshambles, who often performed exhausted, no sleep for days, still f*cked or drunk from the night before, getting 2,000 kids to help them kick a can down the road. Anecdotally, the venue and road crew loved them. But logistically, they knew to stay on their toes, as the Shambles were famous for swerving conventional formalities such as radio promo (Nice. Thanks, lads!) or sound checks (FFS! Thanks, lads ...), often rolling into the venue minutes before hitting the stage. Tonight, as far as the crowd was concerned, they got their money's worth with a filthy, frenetic punk set, leaving all present with sore lungs and dripping with sweat and god knows what other bodily fluids.

When the venue finally pulled the power and put on the house lights to get them offstage (Peter is notoriously hard to get onstage but sometimes even harder to get off, especially if he's told there's a fine for breaching a curfew — I kinda love him for that), we bolted back to the hotel where I planned to unwind, take a bath, then find the right moment to talk Peter into returning my tights (he was labouring under the misapprehension that they looked better on him, even though we can all agree I have much better legs. Right guys?). Shortly after reaching the sanctuary of my room and slipping into a bathrobe, I heard a strange noise coming from the hallway.

Facing page and page 169:
Fun and frolics on tour, in Scotland and beyond.

...

Every atom of my intuition told me not to, but against my better judgment I decided to investigate, only to be faced with what could charitably be described as fresh hell.

Peter and Mick were dragging an unconscious body wrapped in a sheet through the hall. To my horror, just as I opened the door a limb fell lifelessly from the makeshift cocoon.

I believe my exact words were 'what - the - f*ck ...' as I froze, aghast.

With a calmness that belied the severity of the scene, Peter looked up and raised a finger to his lips in the international 'shush' sign.

Indignation snapped me out of my catatonic stasis.

Pause.

'Go back inside, Reens,' he suggested, unhelpfully.

Pause.

Peter's gaze wavered unsteadily from mine to his hastily mummified new mate, then slowly back to mine.

'Um, nothing to see here,' he added, optimistically. Still reeling from the evening's stimulus at the Barrowland, my boggling brain strained to massage the information before me into some logical context. Realising it couldn't, as plausible deniability raced through my mind, I subconsciously began scanning my brain for the names of lawyers who may conceivably owe me a favour. Weakly, I mouthed the words 'Is it ... still alive?'

On closer inspection, my moral compass and I were relieved to learn that this unwitting extra from a *Goodfellas* outtake was just a drunk stranger who had collapsed by pure chance outside Mick's room. The chaps were, in fact, endeavouring to relocate the sorry soul to the hotel lobby. Part benevolence, part conditioned aversion to drawing any attention to the vicinity of their rooms.

After checking his pulse (and stifling a laugh when I heard him quietly snoring), I let them continue their conspicuously covert mission. I closed my hotel room door silently, intent on taking an inventory of my hotel minibar and erasing the last 2.6 minutes from my memory. The contents of said minibar, I reasoned, were in the best position to help me do so.

As I nursed a restorative whiskey and reflected on some of my recent life choices, my reverie was interrupted by another commotion, this time from the room next door. The singer from the support band was apparently in the middle of an existential meltdown and — in a pique of postmodern rock star delusion — was attempting to slide a flat-screen television through the narrow opening of his hotel window. Deciding this was definitely Someone Else's Problem, I turned up the Patti Smith record I was playing, put a wet sock over the smoke sensor (tour tips freebie) and, using my own sliver of a window, I smoked the cigarette I'd been saving.

Just another night on tour with this lot.

The Girl in the Band

What She Brings to a Show

Option A: Nothing.

Option B: Two mobile phones, two copies of house keys, two pairs of sunglasses, two pairs of knickers: it's highly probable that you will lose at least one of these items. You must imperatively add:

- Enough connective memory to remember the band lyrics
- A tattoo that clearly indicates your name and surname
- An indelible marker to write down the number of that superb stranger you will encounter (otherwise you will live with regret forever)
- A couple of quid in your bra
- And, ideally, a loyal and responsible friend (the type of character who will set you straight and save your life)

Above and facing page: Official tour uniform: a pair of shades with peacock feathers on your head, a military jacket and a tattoo you're sure to regret.

What She Brings on Tour

Some of you might have a romantic and grandiose idea of what being on tour would be like. Before your mind wanders away to that idyllic fantasy of Kate Hudson in *Almost Famous*, consider this: touring is physically exhausting and mentally draining. Be prepared. Before you board the bus, make sure to pack the following:

- Air freshener
- Hazmat suit
- Hand sanitiser and every bacterial disinfectant known to man
- Birth control: more condoms than Leonardo DiCaprio could use in a year
- Aspirin/pain killers
- The best lawyer you know on retainer
- Body armour
- A water gun
- *The Lord of the Rings* trilogy
- Gas mask
- More champagne than I can drink
- Goggles
- Multivitamins
- A journal and a peacock feather
- And your shrink!

Concert Attire

In terms of an actual look:
- Any old dark-coloured clothing that's **waterproof** and **revealing** enough (don't go overboard with legs and go easy on the cleavage) will do the trick.
- Add an **accessory** that's rather showy or even downright fluorescent, which will allow rescuers to readily identify you after you crowd-surf the mosh pit.
- I usually go with the basic/must-have rocker uniform: **military jacket** or **leather bomber**. Both go really well with either **jeans** or a **little black dress**.
- If you wear shorts or a skirt you can add some full-on **psychedelic tights**.
- I like to jump and dance around at a gig, so I always wear flat comfortable shoes, usually either **Dr. Martens** or a beat-up pair of **Converse**.

`PRO TIP`

Please don't **ever** mumble the words 'I'm with the band'. And always remember that snitches get stitches; what happens on tour stays on tour (except if you're writing a book, then it's fair game).

He helped shape
the sound
of a decade.

Peter
Doherty

FOR THE LONGEST TIME, everything I heard or read about my friend Peter was an unfair portrait of the man I've known for two decades. For a period of about six years (2003–9) the British tabloids couldn't get enough – the well-worn 'bad boy rock star' mould was one he was all too easy to pour into. Those closest to him, however, know a very different person, a highly sensitive and complex artist. And artists, they say, are not peaceful souls. He embodies the age-old conundrum: why are creative people so damn self-destructive? A paradox wrapped in an enigma: to people he barely knows he can be incredibly generous with his time and resources, but to those who populate his day-to-day life, the ones he loves the most, he'll often give nothing at all.

He's a mystery and a contradiction. He's hyper intelligent, unapologetic and at turns a real asshole. But whether you're just passingly intrigued, somewhat curious or genuinely interested by him, he'll capture your imagination. Any real time in his company reveals him to be one of the most gifted raconteurs you'll encounter. His voice never overwhelms a story; his words dexterously define the narrative, making it unique. He helped inform the artist I later became, and in his native British Isles he helped shape the sound of a decade.

Peter in Liverpool, 2004.

LIVERPOOL ... BAR — 15/2/04

WORDSMITH

It was London at the turn of the century. Peter was starting the Libertines; I was starting to model.

We were young, poetic and wild at heart and we were set to change the world. But as Mr Doherty wrote and sang so well, 'the world kicked back a lot f*cking harder'.

The sun was setting on a debauched squat party in Shepherd's Bush. As I ploughed through a pack of punk kids with my friend Stephanie, my eyes fell upon Peter for the first time, wearing what I assume at some point used to be a suit which was now precariously held together with safety pins. He was holding court with his guitar, whispering lyrics and staring into emptiness as he weaved through the crowd, and our eyes met.

After quoting Victorian English lines and attempting to pass them off as his own to me and the throng of squat partygoers, he asked, 'Do you like it?'

'Yes, very much,' I replied. 'So did Emily Dickinson!' He smiled as I exposed his thievery, and introduced himself.

I said, 'Hi, I'm Rini'.

'Chi Chi,' he replied.

Confused, I repeated myself, 'No, Rini!' And rolled my eyes.

'Hi, Chi Chi, I'm Peter. You're going to be my wife one day.'

Looking back, I can't help but wonder what might have happened if I'd acted on my first, perfectly sane and rational impulse to run for the hills — and I don't mean Beverly Hills! Maybe then this chapter would have been more about trundling along on a Swiss mountaintop à la Julie Andrews, and not the *'enfants terribles'*.

But I was intrigued.

As I followed him further into the dilapidated old ruin of a house to a corner he called his office that was filled with old newspapers and piled high with scrap journals and old postcards, he offered me a sip of mouldy wine and lit one of the many cigarette butts that were lying around. Time seemed to slow down and accelerate simultaneously around him; it was like being sucked into another dimension of magical creatures and strange encounters, unsure of where I might end up.

He placed a disk on an old record player. My eyes teared up as I heard the recognisable and distinctive music of Leonard Cohen, *Songs of Love and Hate,* which has shaped my every artistic breath since I was a child.

Familiarity between two strangers followed. As we spoke, his soft recognisable voice made me uncomfortable with the profound truths he wove into sentences. His style was eclectic. He looked like a vagabond orphan from a Dickens novel, yet he was by far the most civilised charlatan I had ever encountered. I was a little unhinged receiving life advice from Tom Sawyer in his crooked top hat, especially as he flirtatiously eyed my legs!

This was the beginning of a chapter that would change my life. It would redefine my perceptions of art and of literature and of love.

We started fooling around with lyrics and verse, rhymes and beats.

I asked him, 'Which would you betray? Your heart, or your fate?'

He answered, 'Which one is this? A romance? Or a tragedy?'

The early days with Peter, in London.

CAT
IN A HAT

After many moons — past the bohemian age of bourgeois comfort and several scandalous years of debauchery, dramatic twists and a couple of engagements — I found myself here. Sitting on the floor of a suite at Claridge's Hotel in London at 9 am on a balmy August morning. The room was depressing me and I needed to get the hell outta dodge.

I sat crying on the floor. Around me, a war zone. Broken furniture, smashed paintings, cigarettes butts and shattered glass framing my tragic collapse.

How exactly had I wound up in this pickle, I hear you ask? Well, if you see a pattern emerging, suffice to say this was a case of the same cucumber, different jar. My boyfriend at the time had decided to throw a party in my room for a rank shower of strangers. After levelling the place and dispatching any alcohol in the minibar, the entourage magically evaporated, including the offending boyfriend. Overwhelmed with the mess of it all, I called Peter, who was my go-to speed dial number when in the midst of a breakdown.

The enthusiastic tone in his voice when he picked up gave the impression he was out strolling, a skip in his step and his hair in a braid. In fact, he was in transit to headline at the V Festival in Chelmsford with Babyshambles. The minute he heard my voice, he knew that something was wrong; before I could catch my breath and tell him what had happened, I heard him tell the driver to turn the car back around.

'Just stay there, I'm coming to get you,' he said in a soft voice.

The next thing I knew, Peter was suddenly outside my room. Inconspicuous as ever, there he stood sporting a nineteenth-century cape and holding a top hat that was currently providing temporary lodgings to five kittens.

I had jumped, it would appear, from the frying pan into the fire. Not only was the room trashed, but now I had Peter Doherty and a bunch of crazy kittens thrown into the mix.

To my amazement — and alleviating my growing sense of desperation — Peter sprang into action. He cleaned the room and rearranged the furniture, then ordered me some breakfast via room service. Pointing me in the direction of the shower, he went about packing my suitcase. Doherty had inexplicably turned into Mary freakin' Poppins. As he worked away, the kittens went about the business of unleashing mayhem in various corners of the room, scaling the antique curtains and urinating liberally on anything expensive they found. Meh. You win some, you lose some. Emerging from the shower in a bathrobe, I was presented with a glass of fresh orange juice and a coffee. A scene I found almost disconcertingly civilised, until I forked a piece of bacon only to have the rasher seized by one of the errant cats before it reached my mouth. A shift from the chaos that set us both laughing.

Partners in crime: snapshots throughout the years.

I've had a perfectly wonderful evening, but this wasn't it.

Attributed to Groucho Marx

Digestive and nervous systems partially restored, I began the herculean task of deciding what to wear. Somehow none of my 1930s floaty vintage dresses, nor the whole Balenciaga resort collection (why I had these with me is another story) seemed to tickle my fancy. So, in a moment of divine inspiration (or possibly diminished cognitive faculty), I decided to wear all of the dresses at the same time. This stroke of genius, I noticed, created a mille-feuille-like optical illusion that I fancied passed for avant-garde. Or avant-guard, more likely. I added a belt, boots, my leather bomber jacket and — for the final nail in this insane masterpiece — Peter's woollen scarf. In a sweltering heatwave. As I squinted at my creation of sartorial gibberish in the full-length mirror, I began to suspect I may still be drunk.

Peter took one look at me, nodded a silent 'OK' in sage understanding, then added a pair of sunglasses to my face. Apparently there was something awry with my eyes. They appeared, he explained softly, to be attempting to liberate themselves from their parent sockets. After walking into a door frame,

I reasoned with him I couldn't see a damn thing and if he wanted me to make it to Chelmsford without a liberal smattering of bruises about my person (that he might later need to explain), then best we substitute the shades for some species of hat? Happily we found one in which the rim came far enough down my face to render my eyes secondary to proceedings. I looked like a cross between Jackie Onassis and Audrey Hepburn, if drawn by Tim Burton.

Using the might of our combined negotiating skills we coaxed the five kittens back into the top hat, and with the frozen smiles of Bonnie and Clyde we made our way from the crime of the scene. Directly as we hit the pavement, though, I began melting under the weight of my layered experiment, and my hat fell well below my line of vision. Pulling it up I saw Peter drop my suitcase and start chasing the kittens, who had decided that, on reflection, hat life wasn't really for them. My heart sank further as we were then surrounded by a gaggle of hysterical paparazzi that had been waiting outside the hotel. They got their flashbulbs' worth that day.

Incidents involving daring adventures — from home to motel to Claridge's (top right).

Blazer + Fedora

Peter's style is a melting pot of references. Tall and handsome in a unique way, he looks great in a variety of aesthetics: punk, mod, skinhead, Dickensian troubadour – the list goes on. Arguably though, most of us picture Mr Doherty in his signature garb, which conjures up the spirit of a Victorian nomad à la Rimbaud. This look doffs its cap (no pun intended) to Leonard Cohen's silhouette with a pinch of street-dwelling anarchist. Think dark and moody palettes, with gothic layering. Peter channels his literary heroes with unmistakable sincerity, often introducing a private poetic symbolism into his personal style. He always finds ways to disturb his poor blazer, by wearing a Victorian round-collar shirt underneath (also done by Carven in the 1960s) or a striped Picasso T-shirt, for example. Needless to say, touches such as these have endeared him to those eagle-eyed observers in both the music and fashion worlds who recognise and appreciate authenticity, and his effortless embodiment of the low-key bohemian is singular.

He's been known to surprise us too, with wild and daring combinations that vary from splashes of colour to full-on pink suits, their glam and/or smartness often leaning punk – held together with safety pins, mixed with random textures or broken up by a sea of trinkets. In order to recreate the elusive PD look, let's imagine that you're off to visit your grandma. Eager to impress, you don your best suit, a nice crisp white shirt, a skinny silk tie (complete with schoolboy knot) and a classic wide-brimmed fedora hat.

Over the course of your visit, however, your nana's mind being not quite what it once was, she starts enthusiastically festooning you with the contents of her jewellery box. With a tender eye and patient heart you honour her, and soon you're wearing a selection of her rosary beads, rings, brooches and an array of scarves left in her care that once belonged to your famous Aunty Arthur. All the while, though, you've been knocking back every sherry she offers you, so by the time you say your farewells, you've clean forgotten you've got them on at all. In a fittingly anachronistic twist of fate, on your way back home, your bicycle chain snaps on a remote dark road and you're forced to track through some dense and muddy woods, where you end up being chased by a pack of wolves. (Yes, you live in wolf country. Your gran did warn you of the folly of circulating on a bike.) Eventually, after shaking the pack by traversing some treacherous rapids, you manage to find your way to a secluded petrol station. You have now recreated Peter's signature look. Handsome, unique and chic, but dishevelled in an awesomely apocalyptic fashion.

When The Libertines and Babyshambles exploded, it's difficult to overstate the influence Peter had on fashion throughout those years. Often a successful look comes from a musician taking what's happening in the fashion world at the time and making it his own. With young Peter, it was more a case of a boy doing his own thing, and the fashion world taking it and making it their own. No mean feat! Mr P. Doherty Jr, take a bow.

Peter's trademark stage look: suit? fedora? Check.

Portrait by Philip Gay for
Zoo Magazine,
S/S 2008, issue no. 19.

Post-Arrest
Wardrobe Change

Being fashion-conscious also means being prepared for all eventualities, so – no matter what life throws at you – you're ready to confront it in style.

Having a change of outfit and extra accessories on hand requires planning. I can personally attest, through a vale of lingering post-traumatic stress, that there was a chaotic period in my life when I learned not to get caught empty handed, hoping for the best. When you're engaged to Peter Doherty, you prepare for the worst, 'cause the probability of things going terribly wrong is extremely high.

Layering multiple dresses on top of each other is a practical way to have a wardrobe change on hand without the required state-of-the-art gear in the event that you find yourself in a less-than-ideal situation, such as a police interrogation room (for example). When all other makeover options have run dry, you can still bedazzle your way to looking smart and on fleek for that perfect mug shot!

PRO TIP

Don't sleep with your bandmates: it didn't work for Fleetwood Mac and it's not going to work for you.

Peter accessorising.

The Russian Doll
Art of Layering

- Start with underwear (you do not want to be caught without them).
- A pair of tights or leggings, depending on the season (if you choose socks, always have an extra pair on hand).
- A pair of waterproof boots or comfortable trainers.
- Then add two or three dresses; start with the short, fitted one and work your way up to a floaty, hippy, maxi accoutrement.
- Stroll gently until the fits flow nicely.
- Add a belt, several necklaces, a ring, an oversized blazer and, for the finishing touch, a long raincoat.
- For those of the superstitious variety, add some holy water and a wooden stick to your go bag.

Hedi does not play
to the gallery,
and does not give
a f*ck what you
think.

Hedi Slimane

A gentle punk at heart,
there's a stillness in his art
and a silence in his poetry.

HEDI HAS ALWAYS MARCHED TO THE BEAT **OF HIS OWN DRUM.** He has an internal radar for what's hip and relevant and an innate nose for what the cool kids want to wear. His aerials remain tuned in to the mysterious radio waves broadcast from various underground art scenes. Crucially, he uses these powers (seemingly effortlessly) to transform streetwear into high fashion.

There is nothing mundane in the creation of his collections. I've long marvelled at the complicity of his style choices; outrageous original pieces and strange silhouettes seem like old acquaintances, and familiar vintage references are redefined as something fresh and new.

Hedi remains loyal to his artistic essence. He'll never compromise his style to conform to the establishment, nor will he ever cater to the masses or wish to appease his critics. In short, Hedi does not play to the gallery, and does not give a f*ck what you think.

Throughout his photographs, especially his celebrated black and white portraits, he captures the essence of his subjects with subtlety and fluency, reflected sometimes in the gentleness of an uncommon gesture that reveals one's peculiar soul, in a style that's immediately recognisable as his own.

Portrait of Hedi Slimane.

EAST LONDON, EARLY 2000S

There were still a few traces of modern civilisation visible over grey skies, and we'd scatter poems in the gutter as we'd roam the misty cobbled roads.

I often heard Hedi's name echo through Hackney's back alleys.

We had the same proclivities in life back then, hung around the same squats and shared a penchant for lover boys who were up to no good.

While his high fashion peers were parading around with their bowler hats and their pot bellies pregnant with respectability, Hedi, a charming and handsome French man, dressed in black with a discreet yet vibrant personality, started snapping photos with his trusted Leica camera of boys in bands.

His appetite for raw living quickly earned him a special rapport with musicians, and this trust enabled him to take the kind of candid shots unobtainable to other photographers.

Hedi is always calm and present. He listens. He observes. His discerning eye and his ability to capture true emotion in his subjects affords the rest of us a rare window into their souls.

Like many of the greats, Hedi recognised that music is a skeleton key to most street subcultures, and the beautiful and complex characters that stalked the streets of Dalston, Bethnal Green and Whitechapel with smoulderingly androgynous allure at the time later came to inspire his unique silhouettes.

Which brings me to my favourite aspect about him - he was always on the hunt for new talent. He remained loyal to his humble beginnings, favouring his friends and band of misfits so much that the front rows at his shows were often filled with a motley crew of debauched punks, leaving even the most esteemed *Vogue* editors scrambling for a seat.

Between snapping shots, with a sparkle in his eye or a cheeky smile we would share a laugh over a subtle sarcastic joke that was tragically oh so French.

We often bumped into each other trying to get Peter to a gig or trying to find Peter for a gig. I used to spy on Hedi working from the corners of the Albion Rooms in my long bathrobe and uncomfortable shoes. As the lights went down and the boys began to play, the flash of his camera was a reassuring synchronicity in the often chaotic darkness.

At The Albion Rooms, Margate, UK.

Skinny jeans
by Lucy Pinter for
Superfine, photographed
by Jan Welters.

Skinny Jeans

Is there a secret to the perfect rock 'n' roll look sought by stylists, toffs and teenagers everywhere?

To address this perennial question, come with me as we take a wistful look back to 2004. This was the time when Hedi first worked his magic for Dior and took an underground trend kicking and screaming into the mainstream. Its beginnings were humble – on the backstreets of London and Paris it crept up through the crevices of squeaky-floored indie clubs before exploding into a worldwide phenomenon, ubiquitous in cities and suburbs everywhere. Suddenly every boy in a band began squeezing his butt into jeans so tight that he couldn't run or bend over if his life depended on it.

If you're seeking a contraceptive more efficient than a chastity belt, you should definitely consider uber-tight jeans. The wearer must not only be mindful of circulation failure below the hip, but also the secondary fact that the laborious process of removing them is an excruciating procedure that can easily result in injury. The manoeuvre can require assistance; if indeed one can enlist the services of a sober bandmate/tech, or even two or three – the more the merrier!

Leather Jacket

The Official
Rocker Uniform

1 Crazy hair that says 'I just got out of bed' or 'I walked backwards through a hedge', foliage optional.

2 The oversized leather coat or jacket.

3 Skinny jeans.

4 Optional: Vaseline on the face à la The Libertines to highlight those cheekbones (also useful for a plethora of other things, including removal of said jeans at the evening's conclusion). Although fitting that Vaseline pot discreetly in one's pocket may pose a challenge (they do sell small tins now, perhaps for this reason).

This was the identikit look a girl was faced with when visiting London clubs like Trash or The End around that time. Granted, the boys kinda looked like they'd come to a Halloween party dressed as Joey Ramone, but it worked. There was something incredibly relevant in their nostalgic wink. In short, it's the attitude that makes the look. That's why the faithful can tell whether that leather jacket is your real skin or not.

The secret to a rock 'n' roll look is that there isn't one. Allow me to elaborate.

Observing first-hand how this look percolated from dingy clubs up to high fashion, then from high street fashion to the man on the street, it's clear that perfection ain't the goal, nor is looking pretty. Like skinny jeans, being comfortable is definitely not the goal either.

It's confidence. It's casual sex appeal (without overt sexualisation). It's the irreverence of accidentally telling the world 'I don't give a f*ck' without moving your lips.

It's an attitude, the ever evolving balance of harmony and chaos; from Jim Morrison in his flares to the Sex Pistols wearing bin bags and safety pins.

Rock 'n' roll ain't a fad, nor is it a trend. It's a mindset. Sure, there are those who wing it – even a blind squirrel stumbles on a nut from time to time. But delve into its rich culture and history and you'll be rewarded with a veritable wormhole of inspiration. Not to mention it's also a great use of after school/leisure time … it sure was for me! I used to save up

all my money for records and old books, discovering the works of Mick Rock or Jim Marshall and Bob Gruen. They blew my mind.

You guys don't even have to do all of that. You can just google them.

So to clarify, if you want that iconic rock 'n' roll look, it's not enough to just don the uniform. Adjust your demeanour to the sun culture's temperament, inside and out. The learning of which requires perseverance and fearlessness.

Still not sure? I can make a suggestion.

If you have the courage and the necessary time, hang out on weekends in English pubs. Forget Greece or Indonesia this summer; head instead to Manchester, Liverpool or Dublin, where the elusive genus of the original 2004 indie urchin still survives, under rocks and in dingy bars. Nothing better than observing the species in its natural habitat. Study their movements, scrutinise their way of speaking and decipher their world view, such as it is. Marching penguins have nothing on moshing indie kids.

There is no better proof of the permanence of a trend than the rock 'n' roll silhouettes created by Hedi, whether at Dior Homme, at Saint Laurent or now at Céline.

Like a true master he makes it look easy but don't be fooled by the apparent simplicity; he has spent over twenty years tirelessly and relentlessly reworking this 'rock silhouette', with the elegance that only an artist at the top of their game can muster.

Above: Sometimes all you need is a leather jacket.

Pages 192–93: Moments on tour, en route to Arcadia, captured by Sally. Background portrait by Jen Carey.

Amy Winehouse, photographed by Bryan Adams for *Jalouse*, Paris, 25 January 2008.

AMY WINEHOUSE
AND
MARK RONSON

Well, I remember you well, in [some old] hotel,
You were [happy], your heart was a legend

Adapted from 'Chelsea Hotel No. 2'
by Leonard Cohen

AMY WINEHOUSE BEGAN WOWING THE WORLD WITH HER RAW MUSICAL TALENT when she burst onto the scene with her 2003 debut album *Frank*. But as I recall, it was somewhere between the release of her groundbreaking second record *Back to Black* when we started seeing what we now think of as the iconic Amy look. I never spoke to her specifically about it, but I get the feeling that after *Frank* she decided to ignore the stylists hired by her label and just started wearing what she wanted. I heard her quoted once as saying, 'I'm like an old Jewish man. I dress like it's still the '50s.' As much as this is a classic example of her sense of humour, it's only partly true. Her signature beehive, heavy eyeliner, skin-tight dresses and skirts are all nods to her love of the enduring fashion side of rockabilly. But she combined these with more contemporary mod elements such as Fred Perry polos, more popular with the burgeoning London indie scene than the new jazz look I suspect they made her go with for her early photo shoots. I remember first seeing her famous beehive hairstyle – wrapped in a scarf tied in a bow to one side – as she was kicking everyone's asses at pool down at The Good Mixer in Camden, about a year before *Back to Black* came out. When I told her it looked badass, she smiled and shrugged. 'I'm just doing what I want from now on. Plus, it makes me look taller, *innit.*'

That same quiet resolution to be honest was certainly evident in the lyrics on *Back to Black*. I could talk about how her vocal inflections and note choice were beautifully influenced by Billie Holiday, Ella Fitzgerald and the jazz greats she grew up listening to, but ultimately her naked honesty was what set her apart as an artist. She was a gloriously scrappy, working-class indie kid from Camden who happened to have the soul of jazz coursing through her veins. So let's raise a glass to Amy and take a little dive into the Winehouse wardrobe, shall we?

Amy performing at the 2007 MTV Europe Music Awards at Olympiahalle in Munich, 1 November 2007.

IN THE KITCHEN

I first met Amy in 2005 in a London pub over a pint surrounded by the usual rogue's gallery of nefarious ne'er-do-wells that tend to populate the East End's backstreet boozers. Soon after we broke the liquor law with the Lord, our Guinness-fuelled conversation became too difficult to maintain over the increasingly frenetic thrum of the boozer's background noise (if you've ever been drinking in London you'll have noticed how much louder it gets as closing time approaches), but we were enjoying that 'I've just made a new like-minded mate' feeling too much to call it a night so we absconded to a friend's house party nearby. To add a little context: I had no previous knowledge of her, as it was shortly before the release of *Back to Black* and her subsequent catapult into superstardom. That being said, on the strength of this night I might've guessed she was destined for big things, this joyously arrogant Camdenite who bafflingly knew so much about jazz.

We decided to plot up in the kitchen next to the fridge, where Amy had just crammed a pack of Stella we'd bought en route from the pub ('saves a journey *dunnit*?'). By the time the party got going we were already seeing who could remember the most Leonard Cohen lyrics verbatim. She could've written a thesis on the intricate meanings of 'The Stranger Song' and 'The Story of Isaac'. As you can imagine with Amy, this soon meant there were more people in the kitchen than the living room.

By the time we'd drained the last beer we were dissecting the polyrhythms present on the Miles Davis/John Coltrane *Live in Stockholm 1960* performance, demonstrating with pots and pans. This method was extremely effective for clearing out the room! Needless to say, the host of the party intervened before his neighbours did. If you ever read this, London house party guy, soz.

We got to hang out quite a bit after that night, and despite the drama that seemed to follow her around, it never seemed to dampen her joie de vivre, her mischievously playful spirit. She was clever and wise and so very bright; half sugar, half spice. And without question she was always fun! Our fashion senses landed at different ends of the scale: she was on her new feisty rockabilly vibe with figure-hugging skirts and jeans, while as a model I had grown to prefer hiding my body on my downtime, wearing flowy hippy dresses and such. She'd tease me about it, saying, 'Come on, Rinipops, show off those curves, love.' What bloody curves?

She was shocked that I didn't own a bra, to which I'd reply, 'Would you wear socks if you had no feet?' She was always kind to me. She'd fix my eyeliner when I cried, and in those days I cried a lot. But we always ended up back in the kitchen, discussing the meaning of life and its reasons, over tea and crumpets, butter and biscuits. She loved every mistake in the English language, calling them the fate of the poetic gender.

Top: Adventures with Amy and Sally at Sturmy House in Wiltshire, UK.
Bottom: Amy out and about in Camden, London, 24 July 2007.

She'd spend time at Peter's country house, bobbing over to write a song, or try to. When the muse takes him Peter can be more industrious than anyone, but when he doesn't feel like working he's a master procrastinator. One such weekend he tried to distract her with a house tour and a list of plans and schemes, but she was straight down to business. She grabbed a guitar and started strumming something lovely while he buzzed around. 'For f*ck's sake, Peter, come on!' 'Head up a skirt, he's got no time for work' was the prescient lyric Sally contributed to this particular effort.

Those days when we'd all decamp to Peter's country pile for long weekends were legendary. Amy would come over for the weekend, which turned into five days and felt like five weeks. A city girl not likely to allow creature comforts to compromise how she presented herself, Amy would strut about looking fabulous in a 1960s mini skirt, her signature demure black corset adeptly angled to strategically cover her perfect boobs, her signature Cleopatra eyeliner on fleek and beehive perfectly coiffed (though it must be said that over the course of a weekend that thing would get incrementally smaller and we'd find her hair in the most random places around the house).

One of the best things about Amy was how hilariously funny she was, and in moments of pique she never suppressed the urge to unleash a formidably formed string of obscenities. She would just let the filth fly; she could make a sailor blush! They say swearing betrays a lack of vocabulary, but I'm not sure I've ever heard such creative use of the English language as when Amy felt the need to express herself. I felt the full brunt of this particular talent of hers (Napoleon syndrome) when I drew the short straw for who was going to wake her up when she fell asleep on the sofa, as it was winter and we wanted to get her to the warmth of a bed. The volley of abuse was so inspired I ended up laughing so hard I had to sit down myself. Where's a Dictaphone when you need one?

Mostly, all Amy wanted to do was write songs and play music. A prolific lyricist, the quality and spontaneity of her work left anyone who collaborated with her in no doubt that she was on another level. She had such a high rhythm of output that she didn't quite understand when someone couldn't keep up, and would get frustrated when other troubadours lost focus. It always seemed she was on a mission and there was no time to waste.

After one debauched weekend, she left the premises a lot more dishevelled than when she came in, making a Shakespearean exit that would have left any theatre critic asking for an encore. Standing by the door, barefoot, her once perfect coif down to about three strands of hair, she grabbed two of Peter's kittens lurking on the floor and majestically declared, 'I'm leaving now, you f*cking nitwits, and I'm taking the cats with me.'

Cue the wind slamming the door behind her.

Top: Amy looking out of the window of her North London home, 11 June 2008.
Bottom: Peter at his country house in Wiltshire, UK.

Rockabilly Punk-Soul

The 1950s Dress
Giant Beehive
Dangerous Eyeliner

Punk Rock
+ Northern Soul Mix Tape

Amy certainly wasn't the first musician to blend elements of soul with gutter punk attitude; from Dexys Midnight Runners' squatter chic to The Style Council's immaculate suits on one side of the Atlantic, and from Betty Davis's hot pants to Beth Ditto's block-print trouser suits on the other, melding elements of soul and punk has been around for an age. Northern soul's female fashion informed a lot of what became canon for British mod women's wear, which in turn was heavily appropriated by punk chicks across the world. So you see, punk and soul styles are less of a juxtaposition and more two sides of the same coin.

In Amy's case, her heavy winged eye makeup, prison tattoos and sneering attitude did the heavy lifting for the 'punk' side of the equation. I can't reasonably recommend you get yourself down to the tattoo shop or contort your lip for an entire evening, so let's have a look at a few staples that will echo Amy's rockabilly-punk–soul sister style.

Amy performing on the main stage at T in the Park, Balado, Kinross-shire, Scotland, on 13 July 2008.

1 Skin-tight, leg-skimming dresses and skirts: Amy wore these classics in her go-to patterns – floral print or chequers and lace – or straight-up black variations. Pair with visible red bra straps and a wide buckled belt round your midriff and you're good to go.

2 Hot pants, cropped leather jackets and vests: Kicking more towards the punk side of the scale, these were three of Amy's sartorial favourites. While they all go well together, she'd often mix them up with more classic soul elements like mini skirts or round off the punk edges by wearing roses in her hair or high heels.

3 The polo shirt: No Amy style tip would be complete without a mention of this humble staple, beloved by punks, mods, skins, indie kids and northern soul aficionados alike. Amy looked amazing in a simple Fred Perry polo shirt – frankly, I've always thought they were better suited to girls than boys. Versatile too, they work well with most things in your wardrobe.

PRO TIP

As always, combine the above elements with your own style. If you go full-Amy all of a sudden you're going to find yourself answering some questions down the pub. If you, too, admire her fashion, embrace her essence and weave some elements into your look. Have fun with it!

Mark Ronson

MARK'S STORY IS ONE OF REMARKABLE SUCCESS, going from a renowned hip-hop DJ in his youth to a seven-time Grammy Award-winning artist and producer. He moved to New York from London at age eight, and by the time he was sixteen he'd become a fan of Run-DMC, Beastie Boys and A Tribe Called Quest. By the late 1990s Mark had already made a name for himself on the decks of the right clubs and parties.

His stellar career is only surpassed by his impressive résumé; he has an incredible collection of little statuettes – Oscars, Grammys, Golden Globes, Brit Awards and El Flamenco, a colourful little trophy he picked up in Seville while moonlighting as a flamenco dancer. That's right, the boy can cut a rug!

'Markipidia' is my main trusted source for anything funk, soul or go-go related. Mark was once an honorary (if involuntary) member of Operation Juliette, my band with Sean Lennon. When we'd perform our experimental, improvised gigs in run-down venues and random restaurants around the world, Mark would not only show up and encourage our madness, but he'd often climb onstage and roll up his sleeves with whatever instruments weren't being used. He's an extraordinary musician who's self-taught and plays every instrument known to man. (When I'm drunk I'm often convinced I can play drums and guitar. Turns out I can't, as Mark delicately points out while I'm in the midst of one of my gibberish guitar jams. He gives me a look and asks, 'You alright there, Charlie Chaplin?' That's usually my cue to stop traumatising innocent bystanders.)

Mark Ronson
by Stas Komarovski for
Vanity Fair, April 2019

Mark also invented the term 'Riniism', the given nomenclature for the medical condition from which I (and therefore those around me) suffer: a form of spoonerism where I mangle sayings or unwittingly pretzel syllables to create unlikely portmanteaus. For example, when two people meet and immediately enjoy each other's company, I thought the expression was 'they got on like a horse on fire', which I always thought seemed a bit mean. It took thirty-five years for someone to have the decency to correct me.

He's a roguishly handsome, nerdishly talented maestro who happens to be an undeniably kind, sweet and caring human being who sees magic in people and knows exactly how to massage it out of them, often without them even noticing. A talent shared, bizarrely, by the best football coaches and music producers.

Mark is charismatic and funny, and also deeply knowledgeable about music. Combine this with an innate ability to recognise talent and it's no wonder he was soon producing young artists like our beloved Amy Winehouse, for whom he produced 2006's *Back to Black*. Amy also sang on one of my favourite jams, Mark's version of The Zutons' 'Valerie' that, no surprise, became a runaway hit.

On top of his incredible musical output, he gives back through his work with the Amy Winehouse Foundation, Hope and Homes for Children and the national Turnaround Arts program of the John F. Kennedy Center for the Performing Arts, where he is an artist mentor. To quote one of his favourite movies: 'What an asshole'.

The Turtleneck

I've known Mark for years; his quietly intelligent yet childlike charm is endearing. As for his threads, he's been known to rock crazy colours and shiny suits. Another pair of Ronson staples are the ubiquitous sunglasses and the turtleneck.

Mark may well be the most famous contemporary turtleneck jumper fan, sometimes tweeting facts about them, such as this pearl from December 2019: 'Did you know turtlenecks date back to the 15th century? And in Australia, they're referred to as skivvys?!? In America, skivvys are underwear… That's crazy'. Turtlenecks may divide opinion, but taken in a historical context they evoke the black and white portraits of twentieth-century jazz greats, which is possibly where Mark took inspiration. Love them or loathe them, it's undeniable that Mark makes them work, more often than not combining a black turtleneck with a slim cut two-piece suit.

Mark in a signature turtleneck at the European premiere of *Creed* in London, 12 January 2016.

Funk's Influence on Fashion

You don't have to look far to see funk music's impression on the world of fashion, from Funkadelic's stamp on the 1980s catwalk to Prince's influence on Versace. As a slang term, 'funky' is often used to describe an unpredictable style or attitude. Musically 'funk' refers to an aggressive style of dance music driven by syncopated bass lines and drums, combined with multiple instruments all working towards a groove. I find these two definitions of fashion and music pleasingly analogous. Funk music was bold, brave and unique, and has an enduring influence on fashion.

Bring on the Funk

1 Think outside the box. Pick an **unusual piece** that speaks to you and let it be the central inspiration for the rest of your outfit.

2 **Avoid being too match-y.** Finicky ain't funky.

3 Search out naturally **funky brands like Veronica Beard** or **Betsey Johnson** and get creative.

4 Remember, **extreme is good!** An extra-wide belt or an outrageously furry top will get the ball rolling, as will a bold mash-up of prints.

5 Use **unusual colour combinations:** instead of red and blue, try unique mixes like red and purple or brown and blue.

6 Embrace the **asymmetrical**. Off-kilter pieces scream 'Funk Queen'. Vivienne Westwood, while more readily associated with the punk movement, is a master of sartorial asymmetry, especially with her 'Drunken Tailor' range.

PRO TIP

Customise a classic piece yourself by deconstructing a pinstripe shirt or a loud patterned dress.

Facing page: Mark photographed by Stas Komarovski for *Vanity Fair,* April 2019.

Pages 210–11: Mark performing onstage with Amy at the Brit Awards in London, 20 February 2008.

Lindsay Lohan, photographed at home in LA
by Jen Carey and styled by me for *Rika Magazine*.

LINDSAY LOHAN

The Leading Lady

If you obey all the rules you miss all the fun.

Katharine Hepburn

LINDSAY LOHAN IS A LITTLE BIT MARLENE
DIETRICH, a little bit Marilyn Monroe. Somewhere
between that rigorous German work ethic and effervescent
American movie star persona resides her 'spirit animal', a
French caricature that's a combination of Camille Claudel
and Amélie Poulain.

A character who wears her beret in the shower, chain-smokes on
her way to the farmers' market and wakes up most mornings swearing
at her croissants for being too dry. She's an impulsive firecracker,
a fierce student of the human psyche and a sworn enemy of pauses
in conversations. She's a goofball with a razor-sharp sense of humour.

As a child Lindsay started her prolific and sculpted acting career
alongside some of the world's great thespian luminaries. She quietly began
amassing a body of work during her tender and more vulnerable years.

She's half Irish temper and half Italian attitude, which equals
100 percent hotheaded and stubborn. But what makes her a great
actress and above all a formidable human being is her depth and
empathy, the ability to connect with the human condition and the
courage to allow that fragility to move inside her.

Lindsay by Jen Carey.

THE ODD COUPLE

Kate Moss and I were out celebrating my first Italian *Vogue* cover by Steven Meisel at our favourite Japanese bistro in SoHo when, eyeing her messages, she looked up and fluted, 'Hey, why don't we go for drinks with Lindsay Lohan? She's around the corner.'

Being a few sakes in, it took my brain a minute to decode this information, and all I could muster was an image of the twins from *The Parent Trap*. 'Um, OK ...' I managed. Then — waving an unsteady pair of chopsticks at her — I squinted, doubtfully. 'But wait, how old are they?'

We jumped into a car and within minutes pulled up at the entrance of a good old-fashioned East Village dive bar. Lindsay was waiting outside, highly glamorous and very much grown up. To my amazement, there was only one of her.

I'd like to say that I'm saving the story of this legendary night in the company of these two hilarious nitwits for a follow-up book. Sadly, however — much like when Tenacious D couldn't remember the greatest song in the world — I'm afraid I can't remember the mad ramblings of footsteps from this night. Your Honour, cross my heart in a court of law, all I remember from that fateful evening is leaving a strip club at some point and noticing one of my boots was missing a heel.

The resulting way this mishap was making me walk and the hysterical laughter this was provoking in the girls allows the evening's memory to blink back online for five minutes, but that's all I've got. Where are the paparazzi when you need them ... to refresh your memory?

After the mystery surrounding our first hangout, Lindsay and I became true-blue pals in very short order. Our friendship was your classic mismatch: part *Thelma and Louise*, part *The Sisterhood of the Traveling Pants*. Though on reflection I don't think that any of those cats created a secret band (codename: Tibetan Headband), or invented a dance designed specifically to confuse beavers. To the untrained eye we had little in common. She: the all-American bombshell movie star. Me: the awkward goth kid. Sounds like characters from *The Breakfast Club*, right? We couldn't have been more different, but since our infamous lost evening in New York, we still make each other laugh, and on a deeper level we complement each other in a sisterly way: bickering constantly over what to have for dinner, what song to play in the car or what board game to embark on upon returning from a night out. We loved pranking each other and giving each other life advice that somehow we personally couldn't follow. 'You need to take better care of yourself.' Pot calling the kettle black! Or 'I'm telling you, that boy's no good. Stop texting him!' Pot calling the puppy black. And I rest my case!

Clockwise from top left: Attending the Chanel cruise show in LA with Karl Lagerfeld and Lindsay, 18 May 2007; wild nights in NYC with Lindsay, from 2005 to 2011.

···

From the moment our paths crossed, we got on like a house (not horse) on fire, and went with high tempo from mutually being new friend crushes to being legit family. Getting ready to go out was always my favourite part of our nights out together. We'd spend hours carrying clothes back and forth from her residence at the Mercer Hotel to my flat a block away on Wooster Street. Invariably, Lindsay would wind up looking like Rita Hayworth in a sparkling Balmain bustier mini dress with matching La Perla lingerie, body shimmer and stiletto Louboutins. I'd end up looking like Charlie Chaplin on his way to alphabetically ransack a library in a full three-piece suit, tap shoes, granny pants and oversized vintage reading glasses (I reckon my IQ goes up twenty points as soon as I put them on).

I would often see LL scrambling to explain my presence to the club bouncer, who looked confused and tried to politely tell me that I somehow had ventured into a wrong alternate dimension as we were entering the exclusive and coveted VIP room. 'She's with me, she's actually a supermodel!' Lindsay insisted. To which the handsome, strong doorman would answer, 'Yeah sure, and I'm Barbara Bush'. Well guys, Barbara Bush never looked so good!

Wildlings by night and career girls by day, we kept finding ourselves in uncannily surreal situations, from adventures in dance to gambling escapades. We were at least responsible enough to ensure we made it back to HQ by 5 am, as our respective roll calls tended to be 7 am (LL on film sets and me hauling my skinny bum down catwalks); these two sacred hours found us on one of our fire escapes, eating bagels and drinking the remains of yesterday's coffee. As we'd contemplate the NYC sunrise with the strains of Dusty Springfield drifting out our window, we'd cry laughing, telling each other it's going to be another long and brutal day. With a sigh we'd chuck our cigarette butts in our coffee mugs and stumble out to work, and with a fist bump we'd repeat our mantra: 'we'll sleep when we're old'.

NYC shenanigans, captured by BP Fallon, Gavin Doyle and Laura Marie Cieplik.

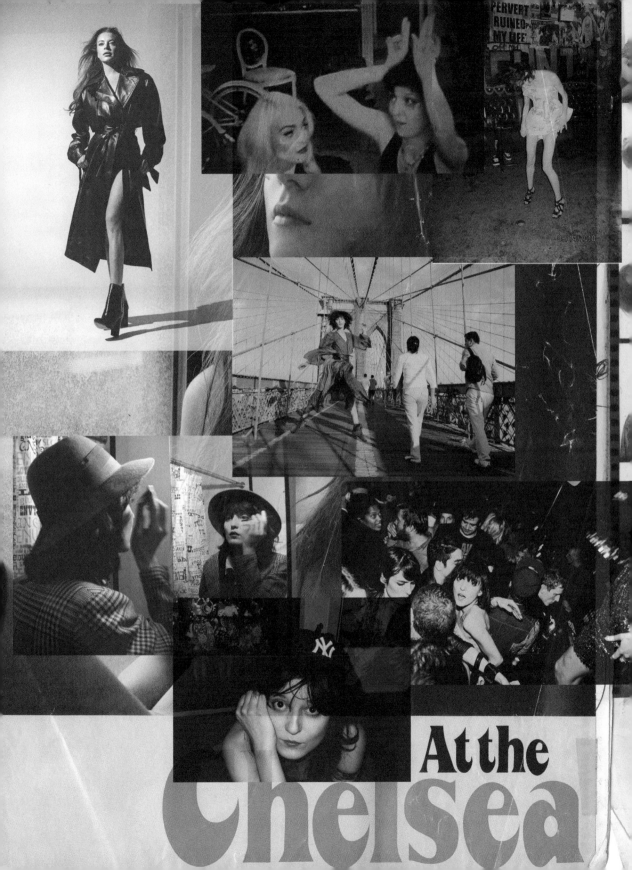

09/14/2010

At the
Chelsea

Lindsay wearing jewellery from her collection.

More is More

Accessories

The right accessory can give even the simplest ensemble a twist. And if you're Lindsay, more is always more in the jewellery department.

When it comes to layering jewellery, LL is the queen of bling, from styling bold necklaces of different lengths to wearing twenty diamond bracelets on one arm while mixing things up with string and candy bracelets on the other.

PRO TIP

Double-bag it: Lindsay never leaves home with fewer than two fully-packed bags, a trick she attributes to what she learned as a Girl Scout: bag 1 is to plan for the best, bag 2 is to prepare for the worst.

At home in Paris, 2004.

Stay Under Cover

Going commando is not a shortcut to happiness. Right under 'Thou shalt not kill' you'll find the oft-ignored sub-commandment 'If thou does, thou shalt cover thine ass'. This rule must be applied in any and all circumstances: brunch, dinner, business meeting, spontaneous coup d'état or fishing expedition. There is no viable excuse or unforeseen reason for you to leave the house without undies.

In the unlikely case of a doomsday scenario, where a meteor might hit the earth and destroy everything in its wake, I'll bet you a slice of mum's apple pie that if you should survive – be you a post office clerk or government delegate – you'll be pleased to have comfortable cottons covering your delicates. Even the zombies in The Walking Dead have the decency to keep things under wraps. Case in point: In the early 2000s, as we entered a new millennium and humanity had just escaped the threat of Y2K, a peculiar phenomenon emerged. The internet was bombarded by pictures of the private parts of celebrities who, by some strange turn of events, refused to wear knickers. Please put it away. Leaving one's imagination to fill in the blanks is the purest form of sexiness. No one needs to see the last turkey in the shop.

What happened? Was there an inexplicable shortage of undergarments in Hollywood, or was the simple fact of covering your bum suddenly outlawed? If so, why didn't the rest of the world get the same memo? We want to know. Or do we? Some mysteries are better left unsolved. I sometimes wonder if that's why Superman wears his underwear outside his pants.

When rushing out the door we recite our mantra for a night on the lash:
✔ Testicles, spectacles, wallet and watch
✔ Credit card, telephone, keys and such.
I'm a firm believer that underwear should feature in this checklist.

PRO TIP

Listen up folks, 'cause this might be the most important style tip in the book: wear some bloody knickers. Just do it!

Old Hollywood Glamour with a Twist

Hollywood is synonymous with celebrity, flashbulbs, glitz and glamour. Before the dark days of tabloid photographers lousing up the dustbins of ex-girl-band members in the 1990s, the designated photo op for stars of the silver screen bloomed organically in the space between opening the limo door and entering a movie premiere. In short order, Hollywood's sharp-minded PR machine soon turned this gauntlet run into global press coverage. A canny move that helped snowball Hollywood's success and reputation as the centre of the sparkling showbiz universe. A ritual that has been refined over the decades to the point where what one wears to cross the few feet from vehicle to velvet rope has become a fashion and press industry subculture all of its own. Just as many people these days only tune in to the Super Bowl to see the adverts and the halftime show, Hollywood events get overshadowed by who wore what, and why they wore it to that movie/ awards ceremony. Think Gaga's meat dress at the MTV Video Music Awards. Or CeeLo Green's 'golden alien' effort at the Grammys. We remember those moments more than who won the awards. There's a small club of women (let's face it, all men really need to do is lay off the carbs for a month and rock up in a tux) who know how to approach the cultural minefield that is the red carpet with apparently effortless style. Zoe Kravitz, for example, is a master of the form.

For my part, I struggled with the red carpet tedium. I'm too impatient. Getting ready for an exclusive event like the Met Gala or the Oscars can take a full day of prep. Skilled stylists help choose from an array of stunning couture gowns; a glam team ensures hair, makeup and nails are on point; and with great consideration – and ideally political tact – some of the world's most beautiful jewellery is chosen. Look like a million dollars while wearing a million dollars.

Others need less guidance. Lindsay, for example, has such an innate sense of style and always looks fabulous for these events. She rarely uses stylists but when she does, she doesn't listen (this is first-hand information, as I've styled her for multiple editorials and found, with equal parts amusement, equal parts professional vertigo, that she's gonna go ahead and wear what she wants).

The overblown artifice and theatre of this ritual came into sharp relief for me when, before one such high-octane, high-stakes event, I ended up doing my own hair and makeup in fifteen minutes and wore a Chanel gown backwards; my accidental/on purpose faux pas caused quite the scandal.

At the CFDA Fashion Awards at the New York Public Library, 4 June 2007.

Red Carpet Countdown

This is the point where I suggest that you fix yourself a cocktail, preferably a martini, and join me as I take you step by step through the complicated and often surreal red carpet boot camp. It could spare your agent a heart attack (sorry, Cheri) and includes some pearls of wisdom that could serve you well on any big day/event.

Day -30: Prep
A month before the event, meet with your stylist to discuss your look. I bet you all think it's going to be easy to find a dress that'll make you look like you're a Greek goddess. You naive fools! It will take longer than one might reasonably assume.
- For starters, consider the colour of the 'red' carpet, which isn't always red! The background colour scheme/story should influence your outfit choice.
- Bear in mind any loyalties or ties you have in place. If you have a contract with a fashion house, you have an obligation to sport their brand. They will likely have a marketing strategy in mind when it comes to dressing their chosen celebrities for an event. It's highly probable that Cate Blanchett and Marion Cotillard or any other actress that has an Oscar will get first dibs from their new collection before you get to make a choice, *mais c'est la vie!* If you don't like it, go to drama school, study hard and become the next Meryl Streep. (FYI, there will never be another Meryl.)

Day -29 to day -5: Care and Feeding
Sleep, drink water, go to the gym, rinse, wash and repeat. Avoid late-night hang-outs, French fries, bread, cocktails or anything that bloats you or has a bad impact on your skin. Basically avoid most things that are tasty or make you feel warm and fuzzy on the inside. You know what those things are! Everything that's remotely fun is forbidden: except sex … that's great for your complexion.

Speaking of food: I never end up eating before events, mostly because I'm always running late, but also because the meals at these things are often prepared by some of the world's best chefs. Nevertheless, for some strange reason no one seems to actually eat at these fashionable gatherings! To my delight, I've been known to go around the table and steal everyone's desserts, so much so that a journalist from *The New York Times* actually wrote a whole article on it: 'Irina Lazareanu had four slices of chocolate cake!' (You can't imagine the outrage!)

Days -4 and -3: Nervous Breakdown
The FedEx package that contained your dream dress is stuck in customs and if, by chance, your stylist is still breathing and somewhat sober, quietly give her a Xanax so she can help you to find a backup option.

Lindsay at the 'Poiret: King of Fashion' gala benefit at the Metropolitan Museum of Art's Costume Institute, 7 May 2007.

Day -2: Small Wonders

Miraculously an outfit arrives (rarely the one you wanted). When you try it on you notice that everyone tries to convince you and themselves that you look gorgeous in it; suddenly the conversation deflects to something so random that you start contemplating the meaning of your existence. The fact remains that the look doesn't fit you and, objectively speaking, you'll need an exceptional seamstress to work overnight to adjust the dress, which is too long, too short or too tight on your body.

Day -1: Accessories to Murder

After you and your whole team (your agent, stylist, mum and a random stranger at the hotel bar) have a proper meltdown and a good cry, everyone agrees that the only way to save your outfit is with the holy miracle of accessorising. This sartorial Jedi mind trick is achieved with a diabolical trifecta of accessories:

- **Shoes:** If said implements of torture are French and they make a sexy sound hitting the pavement, you can't trust a word anyone says – brace yourself for an evening of agony.
- **Jewels:** Add a bunch of diamonds worth more than your mortgage, which may also ruin your night due to the irrational fear of losing one and having to sell your kidneys in order to replace it.
- **Bag:** Oh, and don't forget a clutch so insanely small that you can't fit anything useful in it (including your whiskey flask).

The Big Day: The *Plat de Résistance*!

As long as you adhered to the directives we gave you twenty-nine days ago, you should now be boasting a healthy, radiant glow, ready to light up that carpet like a 4th of July firework. Now comes the time for you to take a leap of faith and blindly put your face in the care of three beauty professionals who you have probably never met, and who start calling you *chérie*, sweetheart and baby from the moment they lay eyes on you. These three strangers will have to form an efficient team in a limited amount of time, under perilous circumstances and your agent's doubtful looks (yes, her again), to transform you into a goddess so you can attract those horny glow bugs known as camera flashes.

Guideline: If it's not fun, keep it basic. Eyes or lips. The more mascara the better.

The good news in all of this is that you can finally stop drinking water now. Downing a minimum of two glasses of champagne is recommended in order to survive this operation without a cerebral trauma when you enter the lion's den, aka red carpet. Stepping on the red carpet, if you see Beyoncé in your vicinity and you're close enough to breathe the same air, do yourself a favour: turn around and just go home.

Facing page: Cinderella leaving the ball.

How to Avoid a Red Carpet Catastrophe
If you somehow find yourself wearing a shepherdess dress
or a chandelier to any event other than Halloween, you
need to stop and do five things:
1. Do not drive.
2. Make sure you're not suffering from a concussion.
3. Make yourself some coffee and sober up, because you're
   probably very drunk.
4. Whatever you do: Do not leave your house like that!
5. Fire your stylist immediately.

Pages 228–29:
Lindsay by Jen Carey.

Sean Lennon and me by Philip Gay
for *Zoo Magazine*, S/S 2008, issue no. 19.

SEAN LENNON

Psychedelic Chic

That was called love for the workers in song
Probably still is for those of them left.

From 'Chelsea Hotel No. 2' by Leonard Cohen

Writing stories in rhyme, sometimes writing stories before their time, like a glimpse into the future, a map of time.

SEAN SINGLE-HANDEDLY RESTORED MY FAITH IN HUMANITY when we met. I'm convinced he's a luminous and magical elf from a faraway galaxy that descended to occupy a mortal body. When you're in his company, reality seems brighter, and life has a tendency to take spontaneous dives down rabbit holes of unbridled mirth, melody and mayhem.

His brain is a sponge that retains random facts and information; you never need to Google anything if Sean's around – he's basically the coolest nerd you'll ever meet. With him, there's never a dull moment. Whether through habit or by design he surrounds himself with the most wonderfully peculiar people. Possessed of a razor-sharp wit and annoyingly fast sense of humour, his buoyant charisma is matched only by a vigorous work ethic; he is, without a doubt, one of the most prolific musicians I've ever met. He has a fascinating method of composing: he first finds a melody and then disconnects the notes from their original cadence to create unexpected but beautiful results. The times I've watched this craftsman's process (whether through collaboration or proximity) were hypnotising. Sometimes he's the effortless architect, rapidly erecting cathedrals of sound with ease. Other times he seems to live inside the songs and tries to devise a way out of reality. Writing stories in rhyme, sometimes writing stories before their time, like a glimpse into the future, a map of time.

And, on a more superficial level, the kid rocks a hat like nobody else.

Sean at the Ritz
Paris for his thirtieth
birthday party, 2005.

THE NIGHT
WE MET: KISMET

The year: 2005. Crisp autumn air blowing golden leaves in eddying thermals through New York's grid of corridors like half-remembered dreams. Our heels playfully swish through the trees' freshly shed foliage. The beauty of autumn in NYC is such; you feel your future in the nostalgia of the past.

The Hollies were playing in the background of a fancy yet dodgy bar/hotel/restaurant where I first met Mr Sean Lennon.

My pal Lindsay Lohan and I bowled in looking fabulously deconstructed, straight from a *10 Magazine* shoot inspired by *Flashdance*. Running on fumes after eighteen hours of acrobatics and not much sleep, food or water, I was in head-to-toe vintage Vivienne Westwood, rocking a curly afro, and in a cloudy yet happy daze.

Lindsay
Hey Sean. This is my friend.

Rini
Heya, Sean.

Sean
Where have you been all my life?

Rini (shrugging)
Stuck in traffic.

As the night unfolded we soon found ourselves in Lindsay's room at the Mercer Hotel. The scene: multiple people dancing with abandon and playing dress-up — floaty dresses, feathers and glitter. I remember feeling a burgeoning new affection in my chest for my brand-new friend

Sean as I watched him haplessly charm everyone, weaving about the party with multiple hats comically and precariously perched atop his beaming and handsome visage.

It was on this infamous Tuesday night that the Tibetan Headbands, our first band, had its genesis. We got the name from my vintage Tibetan boots when — in a flash of inspiration — we repurposed their straps as bandeaux on our heads.

The Tibetan Headbands was more than a band, man. It was a way of life.

Utilising her perennial ability to orchestrate the chaos at these kinds of parties, Lindsay suddenly insisted that Sean and I sit in a corner and write our first song. We laughingly obliged, but within the hour found ourselves looking at each other with a wild surmise.

We're all a bit mad, otherwise we wouldn't have remained friends for so long. But it's the best kind of madness, the creative kind. Maybe it's innate self-preservation, to recognise kindred souls. But that night, for me and Sean, was unmistakably the beginning of a beautiful friendship. It was the fire in which we began to forge armour around ourselves, a bond that helped us both get through the insane situations that were thrust upon us over the coming years.

Around 2 am we heard Lindsay's dulcet tone rising above the happy thrum of the party saying, 'Everyone, listen! Get ready; we're going to my friend's place.' Well, the orchestra must follow the conductor, *n'est-ce pas?* Scrappily we gathered ourselves in our discombobulated

Escapades with Sean, from 2005 to 2007.

and white lights aglow
the Holiday Spirit
week
past
last
somewhe
the

12/06

states and grabbed whatever we could find to cover ourselves and not look weird (weirder?).

Somehow Sean and I ended up in matching pink fur coats (Lindsay was big on having multiple samples of the same garment back then). Jumping into two cars, we drove to a luxurious apartment building in Tribeca.

As we tumbled out of the elevator Lindsay hissed urgently, 'You two! Quick, turn those coats inside out. Mariah hates fur.'

Rini and Sean
Mariah?!?

Where the f*ck were we? As the door opened we heard Mariah Carey's musical trill: 'Darlings, darlings! Come in'.

It felt as if we were entering a different dimension. Mariah greeted everyone individually and attentively, giving Sean a warm hug (of course they knew each other!). After furnishing us with refreshments she proceeded to give us a guided tour of the house, as we followed with eyes out on stalks. By the entrance stood a grand piano, framed with shelves populated by statuettes she dismissed with a bored gesture: Grammys, Billboards, AMAs and such. Her home was elaborately decorated with diverse themes, from Hello Kitty to Marilyn Monroe. She had her own hair and beauty studio to rival any downtown parlour. By and by she led us to her walk-in wardrobe. There was a collective gasp. Spellbound, we followed her into this veritable New York queen's Narnia, a magical land of shiny things and glamour, a dreamland of garments, glitter and rich textures. If heaven has a wardrobe, it looks like Mariah's. By a country mile, though, our favourite room was the one that housed her aquarium. To Ms Carey's amusement and credit, she let Sean and me spend hours with her school of magical fishes. We christened this underwater realm 'Atlantis'. Inspired by these exotic sea creatures and their psychedelic properties, we decided to write a song. With purpose we set out in search of a quiet place and anything resembling a musical instrument.

Sean
I think I remember seeing a little guitar in the Hello Kitty bathroom. Possibly.

Retracing our steps from Mariah's tour we soon found this wonderfully inexplicable shrine to Japan's feline Queen of Cute. Sean tuned a miniature guitar and climbed into the tub where I had plunked myself. He started strumming a chord progression — part Hawaiian, part Gothic. Half sung, half spoken words started to fall from my mouth, rattling around the corners of Sean's guide tones like a pinball in slow motion. Feeling a good song starting to manifest is a bit like seeing a deer near your picnic that hasn't noticed you. You avoid sudden movements, so it doesn't get spooked and run away. After a few times round the chord progression, I sighed, realising at that moment that I was the deer, and that this song had been watching me for some time. As the initially nebulous vowels formed edges and became words, it soon became clear that the lyrics were about Peter. It was a dark time in his life, a time when I couldn't hear his voice any more, a time when he had stopped singing. To me, at least.

One by one
They enter, they sing
And take the sweets that darkness cast
No one knows where the light is going
No one knows where the night is flowing
You used to sing to me,
Of strange places
And silver trees.

Me (looking at Sean)
Perhaps we rhyme because we breathe.

Sean
This song needed no breath. It needed purpose.

Present day, I now remember the subsequent hours we spent in the bathtub like an unapologetically John Hughes-like, idealistic start to a friendship, a beautiful and abstract origin story to the saga that is Sean and me.

With Sean in Paris and NYC, from 2005 to 2010.

Above: With Sean
Lennon and Charlotte
Kemp Muhl at the
Chanel S/S 2010
RTW show at the
Grand Palais, Paris,
6 October 2009.

Facing page: Sporting
a Superfine military
jacket, photographed
by Jan Welters.

Military
Jacket

Music and war don't seem like an obvious
pairing, but the military jacket has become
an iconic uniform staple for musicians for
generations. With its brass buttons and
epaulettes the trimmed silhouette falls
effortlessly, and can be both original and chic.

Japan -Inspired

To subtly reference Sean's unique style, take cues from the classic kimono, the Hello Kitty universe, the *Kawaii* factor and the effortless elegance of its iconic designers.

Comme des Garçons Universe

The summit of Japanese asymmetrical elegance – what the French would refer to as 'absolute chic' – CDG has been pushing the boundaries of conventionality in fashion for a half-century. From their basic black T-shirt to their iconic trainers, CDG designs ramp up the cool factor and are the epitome of the nonchalant aesthetic. Translation: you're so freaking well put together that you literally don't give a toss.

• **The oversized suit**: Think Talking Heads – the *My Girlfriend is Better* video – with the over-the-top jacket and its massive shoulder pads. In this scenario, disproportion is always your friend: go massive on top with trousers that are loose and too long on the bottom. It's all about the attitude while wearing such a garment.

• **Black on black on black:** If you don't want to take risks, play a safe CDG look by adopting the Rei Kawakubo uniform – adjusted black leather perfecto jacket + plain acetate black shades (a good Ray-Ban Wayfarer could work), and a perfectly cut and fringed straight black bob.

The *Kawaii* Factor

You can embellish a simple jean and white T-shirt look by adding a cute Hello Kitty bag, and tie it all together with pink wool socks and a thin, delicate matching belt. The use of bright fluorescent colours can make a dull outfit come to life. Never go over the top with accessories; the fun and playful aspect of the bag makes it enough of a statement piece. The touch of colour with the belt and socks is strategic enough without being overbearing.

Above: My apartment in Paris.

Facing page: Portrait wearing oversized garments in Paris.

Kimono

How to Decipher a Kimono

Kimonos come in various styles, traditionally used for different social occasions and culturally representative of a woman's marital status. Consider the following three styles if you wish to incorporate your dating status into your kimono style. Equally useful if you're wondering which way to swipe on Japanese Tinder.

1 The *furisode* is notable for its longer, larger sleeves that cover the arms to the wrist, with a panel that extends to the ankle, which can be impractical. Apparently sleeves are a way of showing sentiment in the land of the rising sun. I would have opted for the Araki bondage technique, but sadly no one asked me. Traditionally, *furisodes* are for unmarried women and habitually worn to formal occasions. Fundamentally, this style is an unspoken way of advertising that you're ready to get married.

2 The *iromuji* is known as the easiest kimono style to wear; the name literally means 'plain colour': one block colour and no patterns. They come in all colours except black or white and can be worn by anyone from married to unmarried women and everything in between.

3 The *shiromuko* is all white and the most elaborate kind of kimono, worn to traditional weddings. The hem that trails along the floor forms a circle, so the bride needs a team of helpers to walk – which is an excellent excuse if you get plastered on your wedding day.

PRO TIP

The most important element to consider when wearing a kimono in western society is to dress down. For example: pair with ripped baggy jeans, a simple tank top and vintage Converse.

For a more formal approach, combine a white *shiromuko* kimono with tailored black trousers and a pair of chic Saint Laurent high heels. Complete the look with a slick chignon and bright red 'look at me' lipstick.

Facing page: Portrait by Kristin Vicari in London.

Above: In a kimono dress, Paris, 2007.

Pages 244–45: Sean in Paris in 2005.

Yoko Ono by Leslie Kee.

OH, YOKO

Art is my life and my life is art.

Yoko Ono

YOKO ONO IS AN UNDENIABLE FORCE OF NATURE. Blessed with a wild imagination, she is one of the most controversial and influential artists of recent times. Her body of work is as diverse as it is symbolic. Ever the prolific polymath, she's lent her creativity to filmmaking, fine art, song writing and activism.

Having spent a lifetime challenging prescribed conventions of art, she continues to push the limits of our conceptual views while breaking new ground for women in the process. All this despite constantly being forced to navigate an endless storm of criticism from certain corners of a patriarchal society. This she has done with strength, fearlessness and, crucially, love.

Since the 1960s, Yoko's ability to think laterally has been evident in her art work. The world of modern art can sometimes seem intimidating – too conceptual, dense and impenetrable. Yoko's freshness has always been her desire to tear these walls down. Despite filtering reality through her own unique prism, her creations reveal a natural generosity and desire to communicate – abstract, yet accessible. However mysterious or ethereal this otherworldly sorceress may seem, she has made her life's work of revealing the secrets of cryptic language, ones that are rarely exposed – if indeed we take the time to look, feel and listen.

A tireless student of history and numerology, she possesses a youthful curiosity that keeps her seeking answers through both modern and obscure ancient mediums. The untrained eye may see madness in her methods, but her results undeniably prove there is method in her madness.

As a young Japanese woman, Yoko chose a way of life that required more bravery than most of us can ever understand, more than I could possibly begin to touch upon through these few words in this funny little book about clothes. But I can say this – her integrity and resilience have been and will remain a welcome, enduring inspiration to millions like me, and (considering you bought this funny little book about clothes) like you too.

Besides her cast-iron status as a heavyweight icon of modern art, Yoko Ono has long been viewed as an international style icon and a fashion trailblazer. Just hearing her name evokes distinctive haircuts and her mesmerising hats, not to mention the iconic image of the pale white 'bed-in' pyjamas. From her iconic militant ensembles to wearing trainers on her wedding day, her relationship with fashion has always been her own, ever redefining elegance with her attitude.

Facing page: Yoko Ono in her apartment at the Dakota, NYC, 13 November 1982.

THE DAKOTA

I remember that moment perfectly, when I set foot inside the Dakota with Sean to meet Yoko Ono for the first time.

I was so nervous. Yoko had been an inspiration for years. Her way of combining art and activism was something I'd admired since I was a teenager — her 1964 *Cut Piece* is one of my favourite works of performance art.

I felt incredibly grateful to be given a grand tour of this mythical castle in the sky where Yoko resided, and what followed was an awakening for my artistic senses. Art covered the walls (Goya, Magritte, Chagall), musical spirits haunted the halls. Like a child, I followed Sean from room to room, marvelling at each new surprise around every corner.

By the time we got to the white room, I was overwhelmed with emotion. Walking in, we were met by a single ray of light which somehow filled the whole room, covering the walls by making sunshine out of shade. I stood there, spellbound, until Sean sat at his father's piano, breaking the silence with melody and rhythmical breathing.

In between loops and folds
in a time of distortion
by borrowing willing minds
between his fingers and half a sigh

A family picture in an old frame,
held together by Scotch tape
lies next to a paper airplane
by a chalky marker on the wall.
Tip toe around a piece of art
Made by a drop of life
That echoes through the memory hall.

I can still picture it when I close my eyes — every single last detail of that room imprinted on my mind like a photograph.

We continued our exploration throughout the house, each new cosmic curiosity we encountered carrying a story Sean divulged colourfully. At one point I found myself gazing at an Egyptian mummy nestled amid an array of Yoko's pieces. I felt the heart of my essence witness a new lease on destiny.

Eventually Sean's tour led us to the kitchen, where my eyes first fell upon Yoko. You could have knocked me down with a feather. There she was, sipping tea, perched gracefully on a wooden chair, flawless in every way.

Approaching her, I tried to conceal my nervousness. Shyly attempting an introduction, I think I said something daft like 'pleased to make your acquaintance', and reflexively bobbed a curtsey. Thankfully, she quickly put me at ease with a smile and a twinkle of the eye — amused by this clumsy faux pas.

We settled around the kitchen table and, as we poured tea, so too the conversation began to flow. Our thoughts and words began echoing in accord as we touched on the fathomless mysteries of life, art, dreams, and those rare soulmates one sometimes finds for whom still waters run deep, and those who conceal dark landscapes within.

I felt deeply privileged to savour such an unfiltered, creative exchange with one of my heroes. I quickly realised that her understanding of such things as the nonlinear nature of time or the broader purpose of destiny far surpassed my limited knowledge of these philosophical and abstract notions.

Quietly I sat there, absorbing her every word.

To this day I remain humbled to learn from this wise soul, possessed as she ever was of a beautiful and childlike look of wonder in her eyes.

With Yoko and Sean at the Dakota and around town.

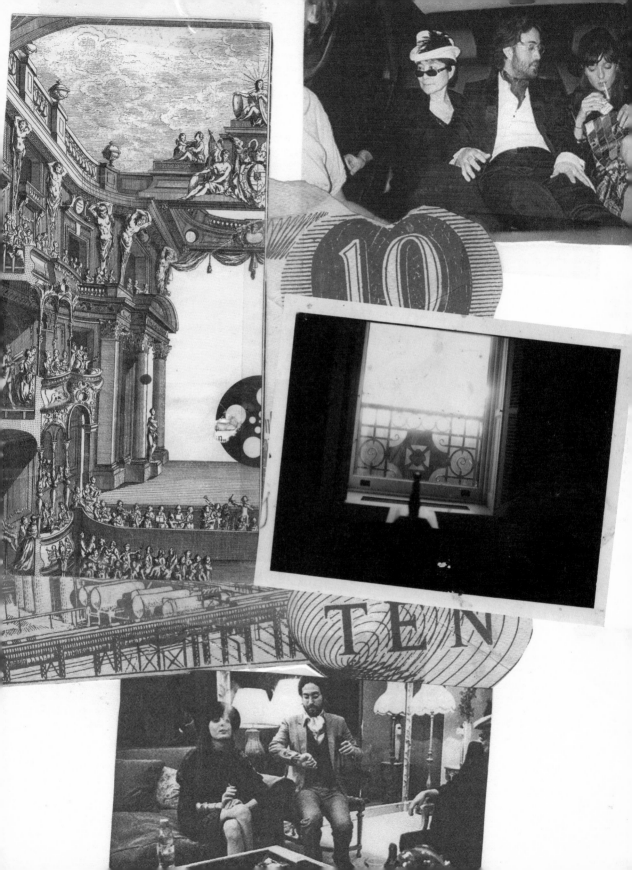

SEAR SOUND STUDIO

Waking from a night of fitful sleep, I leapt out of bed and unsteadily tried to compose myself. Whilst showering I suddenly remembered — lyrics! I frantically grabbed my journals and, with hair still dripping wet, I scoured the apartment for envelopes and napkins on which I'd scribbled little poems and vignettes.

Terrified for once of arriving late, by 8 am I'd fled my SoHo apartment with all the grace of an ambulance driver. I hailed the first cab that passed to take me to the legendary Sear Sound recording studios.

The second I sat in the taxi I felt nauseous. By the time we'd passed Union Square I had to ask the poor cabbie to pull over. He'd barely come to a full stop before I opened the car door and left my breakfast on the pavement. Truth be told, I was overwhelmed with nerves and I don't get nervous that often. But this was no normal day, this was the first recording session for the EP Sean and I had written (time spent here would also yield our first single, and the soundtrack for a Chanel fashion show).

Compounding my nerves was the fact that it was this same studio where twenty-seven years ago John and Yoko started work on their *Double Fantasy* album. Sear Sound NYC was also where Yoko last saw John alive, before he was brutally assassinated in front of their apartment building on 8 December 1980. She hadn't returned here ever since. Today, though, Yoko was in attendance and, I imagined, was greeted by countless fragmented memories echoing through these walls.

When I arrived I found Sean already in the Live Room, setting up the equipment. Recording sessions frequently end up with him — ever the workaholic — playing every single instrument, producing and composing all the music.

While recording, Sean is a man on a mission who knows what he's doing. The studio is very much his wheelhouse and I felt completely out of my depth. Tuning a guitar, Sean glanced up at me and sighed, 'Geez, Rini, you look like hell.' Without missing a beat I shrugged back, 'That's weird, 'cause I feel like crap.'

Within a few hours I found myself confined to the vocal booth tracking my parts while a growing sense of claustrophobia crept over me. My brain was suddenly overrun by a chemical euphoria. Possibly in an attempt to distract from my growing anxiety, I decided to start challenging the necessity for headphones. Righteously punching the talkback button, I demanded to know 'did the Beatles use headphones?! Did the Rolling Stones use headphones?!'

'Yes Reens, they did,' came Sean's patient but deadpan reply. Before I had time to challenge this outrageous hypothesis, Yoko — who until now had assumed a relatively passive role in the control room — came to my rescue. First with soothing words of encouragement and shortly thereafter by pulling focus with hilarious anecdotes that had the engineers and all of us in stitches. I marvelled at how she'd intuitively dialled into my energy. Her genuine spirit maintained a direct link to the world and her spontaneity seemed to undermine the boredom of everyday life! Soon, thanks to her subtle charisma, I had almost forgotten all about my fears and silly insecurities and smoothly completed the song, each take being met with smiles and thumbs up from the other side of the glass.

By lunchtime we'd begun sensing this was to become a very special record. Famished, we fell laughing into the dining area to be met with the biggest surprise of the day: Yoko had prepared the most delicious Japanese meal I've ever tasted! We ate and listened to Yoko's tales from the good old days. Towards the end of the meal, her natural flair for bringing a narrative to life with sounds and props reached a crescendo when two racks of clothes manifested themselves, and before anyone mentioned coffee, we were laughing and playing dress-up.

I quietly noted in awe how Yoko was orchestrating the chaos. Whether by design or by instinct, this bonding ceremony served to lift all our spirits, and we enthusiastically started to enjoy the process when we got back to work.

Clockwise from top left: Making music; two photos of the Sear Sound studio where we recorded in the summer of 2007; at Julian Lennon's *Timeless* photography exhibition premier in 2010; Sean on the piano by Sasha Eisenman; newlyweds John Lennon and Yoko Ono's 'Bed-In For Peace' in Amsterdam in 1969.

Hats

Put a Lid on It

The debate over why icons from the 1960s and 1970s became the pervasive influence on what young people wore for the next half-century rages on. Some scholars assert the reason lies with their association to the sexual revolution; other academics insist it's thanks to said icons' ties with the era-defining liberation of youth and young identity, the casting off of the shackles of convention during totemic moments like Woodstock and Isle of Wight.

My view, however, is an altogether more reasonable one: the enduring power and omnipresence that stars of this era maintain over popular culture and fashion comes down to one thing – hear me out – hats.

The use of flamboyant hats by rock icons to add dramatic flair to a look is a well-evidenced tactic, but Yoko's array of original approaches and imaginative ways to amaze with millinery remain unmatched. (Try saying that when you're sober.) Queen Ono is the proud owner of the most incredible collection of hats, housed in a dedicated room at the Dakota. Hers is a distinctive and intentionally atonal approach to hat wearing, ignoring the conventional harmonies habitually associated with the accessory's use. Like many artists, her clothes are a form of self-expression, and while she seems to favour a well-cut tailored silhouette, punctuation tends to come in the form of a quirky hat. A classic example can be seen in her use of the beret in the epic Iain Macmillan photographs with John – she's wearing short shorts, but the beret

snaps us away from the subtext of 1960s feminist sexual freedom and underlines the militantly pacifistic ethos of the 'War is Over (if you want it)' campaign for peace spearheaded by Yoko and John. See just how much can be said with a simple choice of headwear?

Yoko is a woman who wears many hats, both literally and figuratively. When she enters a room, time stands still. Shadows of gravity-defying feathers start dancing on walls, drawing your eye inexorably towards her extravagant headwear.

On stage, at work, while trying to save the world, or off duty when she's enjoying her daily walks through Central Park, the hat (be it fedora, beret or top hat) is the one constantly variable piece of her personal style.

No matter what *chapeau à plume* tickles your fancy, the question remains when and where we should leave our hats on. According to Laetitia Crahay (one of the most successful hat designers in the world), hats can very well be incorporated into our everyday wardrobe choices; they can give a certain *je ne sais quoi* to a dull, plain outfit. For example, just adding a *joli* beret can elevate your look to *le French chic* status, while simultaneously hiding your dirty hair. Yes, this is a hangover hack that can be applied with most hat choices. You're welcome. Speaking of life hacks, a hat can be an excellent conversation starter if you're looking to make new friends.

PRO TIP

Note to self: if you're not attending the races at Ascot this year, the outlandishly decorative hat may not be for use on any given day. It should only be worn while attending Burning Man or to scare off your mother-in-law when she invites you to lunch.

Military Garb

The 1960s Militant Look

By wearing a green military infantry jacket along with a perfectly placed beret, Yoko was echoing Che Guevara's revolutionary uniform during the give peace a chance anti-war campaign that she and John were heading at the height of the Vietnam War. The commercial use of military or camouflage garments in fashion became very trendy over the years. The most important thing you have to remember when you wear military clothing is to mix it with everyday casual articles:

- A simple tank top or white shirt, blue jeans or black skinny jeans, even shorts in the summer can tone down the outfit so you don't look like you're in the middle of a foreign invasion or a coup d'état when you step out on the town!
- If you're into cargo pants, camouflage or not, the same rules apply: they usually go hand in hand with an oversized jumper (cue the 1990s) and are known to love any basic leather jacket! Please do not go full metal jacket though.When it comes to finding the right shoes for this look, I usually opt for a

ballet flat (I quite like the contrast between the rigid military attire and the idealistic softness of the ballet shoe), but for the more adventurous spirit you can kick it off with a leopard print high heel!

- Always be careful what colours you mix with these kinds of outfits. Green on cucumber green on leprechaun green can be a little overbearing. (Yes! Even on Saint Patrick's Day.) Be mindful to avoid wearing yellow with this look (especially that acidic canary yellow) as it washes you out and can make you look like you need a liver transplant!

From the shoot for John Lennon's *Gimme Some Truth* album, photographed by Iain Macmillan.

The Art of Dressing Up

Unfortunately, most of us lose our childlike imagination when we grow up; sure, some leftover residue of dream-like fantasies still lingers from our youth, but we mostly try to conform to societal norms by mirroring our conventional upbringing. We try to fit in, wanting to belong.

There are some exceptions to this rule. Some rare and fiercely creative spirits who

thankfully aren't afraid to do their own thing. Like any style trailblazer or artistic social movement pioneer, Yoko was often the first to dare to push the envelope on society's narrow packaging. Behind each of her iconic style choices, there's an untold story. Messages left behind in photographs for the willing eye to discover.

Above: Sean and Yoko at the Ritz Paris Coco Chanel suite, 2006.

Facing page: Yoko and John Lennon in Paris for their honeymoon, 23 March 1969.

Pages 258–59: Yoko sitting at the window of her apartment, during an interview in NYC, 28 June 1973.

Conclusion

This book is a portrait of a moment in time: the 2000s, aka the 'noughties'. That funny turn-of-the-century period at the beginning of the new millennium when the spirit of the 1990s was certainly still breathing through music, as its rhythms grew dramatically louder and fashion's grand narrative grew a touch confused.

That singular window in time, before mobile phones and social media started dictating our way of life and our perception of reality. The noughties ... a reflection, in part, of my general attitude during the early 2000s. 'Cause boy was I naughty in the noughties.

To you, who dared to pick up this book, and to you, who is reading these words now: I hope you've enjoyed perusing this book as much as I loved making it. With its trials and tribulations and flickering glimpses of my journals and old photographs held together by the thread of great expectations, I hope you'll have learned a thing or two (beyond the importance of wearing knickers!).

The fashion and music industries have always inspired cultural movements, like parallel rides secretly dictating the look of all of our 'Beat generations'. No matter if you consider your style to be modern or retro, I suggest pouring heaps of 1970s punk into your attitude. Be fearless, loud and daring. Even in uncertain times, always be on the lookout for new adventures, those that brave the heart and set the soul asail.

To the beautiful and complex characters who populate these pages – my collaborators and fellow artists: thank you. You have my eternal gratitude for trusting me with our story and your work. You, who have inspired me and constantly taught me to refuse complacency; you've shaped the way I think, the way I create and the way I choose to live my life. Most importantly, each and every one of you is in some small way responsible for the way that I put my trousers on each morning: one leg at a time, and often backwards.

Yours sincerely,
Irina

Portrait by François
Rotger.

ACKNOWLEDGEMENTS

A very special thank you
to Inez & Vinoodh, who were
the first artists to support
this project, and to:

Bryan Adams
Sally Anchassi
Marie-Catherine Audet
Alex Babahmadi
Balenciaga
Lucy Baxter
Freja Beha
Billy the dog
Lena Bodet
Cheri Bowen
Chris Brenner
Jen Carey
La Maison Chanel
Helena Christensen
Laura Marie Cieplik
Camille Claudel
Leonard Cohen
Lily Cole
Alex Conu
Laetitia Crahay
Sleiman Dayaa
Agyness Deyn
Dior
Peter Doherty
Lily Donaldson
Gavin Doyle
Aurelie Duclos
Victoire Duigou
Anaïs Duquesne
Sasha Eisenman
Edward Enninful
Robert Fairer
BP Fallon
JD Ferguson
Stéphane Feugère
Adam Ficek
Claude-Olivier Four
Philip Gay
Nicolas Ghesquière
Raegan Glazner
Leo Haddad
Lady Amanda Harlech
Shalom Harlow
Harper's Bazaar España
Jonas Herbsman
Simon Hilton

Anna Hoberman
Marc Jacobs
Jalouse
Grace Jones
Mick Jones
Greg Kadel
James Kaliardos
Leslie Kee
Greg Kessler
William Klein
Susan Kohler
Stas Komarovski
Marc Kroop
Diane Kruger
Katarina Kuehl
Karl Lagerfeld
Marc Lamour
Martin Laporte
Gaelle Lassée
Constantin Lazareanu
Viorica Lazareanu
Thierry Le Gouès
Sean Lennon
Anouck Lepère
Angela Lindvall
Lindsay Lohan
Jean-François Loperena
Marie José Loperena
Sophie Loperena
Luigi & Iango
Marie Claire Italy
Audrey Marnay
Kate Mascaro
Drew McConnell
Craig McDean
Alasdair McLellan
Karla Merrifield
Rosalie Miller
Malina Molgan
Celine Mombert
Kate Moss
Anna Mouglalis
Charlotte Kemp Muhl
Carolyn Murphy
Stepanie K. Nihon
Yoko Ono
Lucy Pinter
Sasha Pivovarova
Kirsty Reilly
Hilary Rhoda
Rika Magazine

Mark Ronson
François Rotger
Jed Root
Emanuele Salini
Jonathan Sanchez
Marie-Amelie Sauvé
Venetia Scott
Jason Sharpe
David Sims
Rasmus Skousen
Hedi Slimane
Pennie Smith
Max Snow
Camilla Staerk
Jessica Stam
Jay Stanley
Stephen Mark Sullivan
Emma Summerton
Tank magazine
Joseph Tenni
Michael Thompson
Tasha Tilberg
Topshop
Peter Utz
Versace
Virginie Viard
Kristin Vicari
Visionaire
Rosie Vogel
Vogue Britain team
Gemma Ward
Erin Wasson
Alex Wek
Jan Welters
Mick Whitnall
Harriet Wilson
Amy Winehouse
Olivier Zahm
Carlo Zollo

With deepest thanks
to Pascal Loperena,
my partner in art and
in crime, who was with
me every step of the way
throughout this journey.

In memoriam
Sam Archer and Ruby Rose
Philippe Elkoubi
Hedley McConnell

Photographic Credits

p. 4: Irina Lazareanu archives; p. 5: tl © Jen Carey / *Rika Magazine*; c © François Rotger; all others Irina Lazareanu archives; p. 6: © Jan Welters; p. 9: © Inez & Vinoodh; p. 11: © Jan Welters; p. 12: © Thierry Le Gouès; p. 14: © Robert Fairer; p. 17: © JD Ferguson; p. 18: © Michael Thompson; p. 21: © JD Ferguson; p. 23: bkgd Irina Lazareanu archives; l © Robert Fairer; r © Pool BASSIGNAC / BENAINOUS / Gamma-Rapho via Getty Images; p. 25: bkgd and br Irina Lazareanu archives; t © Victor VIRGILE / Gamma-Rapho via Getty Images; tr © Robert Fairer; p. 26: © Myrna Suarez / Getty Images; p. 27: © Irina Lazareanu; p. 28: © Malina Molgan; p. 29: © Matt Irwin / Trunk Archive; p. 30: © Fernanda Calfat / AFP; p. 31: © Michael Thompson; p. 32: © Jan Welters; p. 33: Irina Lazareanu archives / All rights reserved; p. 35: © Max Snow / *Rika Magazine*; p. 36: © Martin Laporte; p. 37: © Nick Harvey / Wireimage / Getty Images; p. 38–39, 41: Courtesy of Helena Christensen; p. 43: © Inez & Vinoodh; p. 44: © DAVID X PRUTTING / Patrick McMullan via Getty Images; p. 47: © Dan Martensen / Trunk Archive; p. 48, 51: © Sebastian Sabal-Bruce; p. 52–53: bkgd François Rotger; p. 52: 2nd row l © JD Ferguson; 4th row r © Stéphane Feugère; br © Sally Anchassi; all others Irina Lazareanu archives; p. 53: 2nd row c © JD Ferguson; all others Irina Lazareanu archives; p. 54: © Chris Brenner; p. 57: Photo by Paolo Roversi, courtesy of Milla Jovovich; p. 59: bkgd Irina Lazareanu archives; all others © Chris Brenner; p. 61: bkgd Irina Lazareanu archives; cr © DMI / The LIFE Picture Collection/Shutterstock; all others © Chris Brenner; p. 62: © Chris Brenner; p. 63, 64–65: © Jen Carey; p. 66: © Alasdair McLellan / Art Partner; p. 69: © Rose Hartman / Getty Images; p. 71: bkgd Irina Lazareanu archives; t and b © Topshop; p. 73, 75: Irina Lazareanu archives; p. 76: © Ron Galella / Ron Galella Collection via Getty Images; p. 77: © Catherine McGann / Getty Images; p. 79: © Shutterstock; p. 80: © James Devaney / WireImage; p. 81: © Niki Nikolova / FilmMagic / Getty Images; p. 83: © Matt Cardy / AFP; p. 84–85: l All rights reserved; tc © François Rotger / *Marie Claire* Italy, 2008; all others © François Rotger; p. 86: Irina Lazareanu archives; p. 87: © Jan Welters; p. 88–89: © Luigi & Iango / Trunk Archive; p. 90: © William Klein; p. 93: Toni Anne Barson Archive / WireImage; p. 95: bkgd © CHANEL / Dossier de presse Collection Haute Couture Printemps/Été 2007; tl © Robert Fairer; tr and cr © CHANEL / Photographe Karl Lagerfeld / Dossier de presse Collection Métiers d'Art 'Paris–Monte Carlo' 2006/2007; bl © BILLY FARRELL / Patrick McMullan via Getty Images; br © Stéphane Feugère; p. 97: bkgd © CHANEL / Dossier de presse Collection Métiers d'Art 'Paris–Monte Carlo' 2006/2007; tl © Antonio de Moraes Barros Filho / WireImage; tr © David Fisher / Shutterstock; bl Irina Lazareanu archives; br © CHANEL; p. 99: bkgd and br Irina Lazareanu archives; t © Karl Lagerfeld for *Visionaire*, no. 49, courtesy of *Visionaire*; bl © Gavin Doyle; p. 101–3: © CHANEL / Photographe Karl Lagerfeld / Dossier de presse Collection Prêt-à-Porter Printemps/Eté 2007; p. 104–5: © Gavin Doyle; p. 107: © Jan Welters; p. 109: © CHANEL / Photographe Karl Lagerfeld / Dossier de presse Collection Prêt-à-Porter Printemps/Eté 2007; p. 111: Irina Lazareanu archives / All rights reserved; p. 112–13: bkgd © Robert Fairer; p. 112: bl and cr © Robert Fairer; all others Irina Lazareanu archives; p. 113: tl © Robert Fairer; cr and br © JD Ferguson; c © PASCAL LE SEGRETAIN / AFP; all others Irina Lazareanu archives; p. 114: Courtesy of Fairchild Archive; p. 117: © Joe Schildhorn / Patrick McMullan via Getty Images; p. 119: bkgd Irina Lazareanu archives; tr © Robert Fairer; c © Dimitrios Kambouris / WireImage for Marc Jacobs; bl © JOE KOHEN/ AFP; p. 121: bkgd Irina Lazareanu archives; tl and tr © Catwalking / Getty Images; br © FirstVIEW / IMAXtree.com; p. 123: bkgd Irina Lazareanu archives; tr © Leslie Kee; br © Koichi Kamoshida / AFP; p. 125: © Philip Gay; p. 126: © Rasmus Skousen; p. 127–29: © Venetia Scott / Trunk Archive; p. 130: © Nicolas Guérin / Contour by Getty Images; p. 133: © Victor VIRGILE / Gamma-Rapho via Getty Images; p. 135: bkgd and Irina Lazareanu archives; tl © Greg Kessler; tr © Irina Lazareanu & Julia Dunstall - Balenciaga Campaign Spring Summer 2006 - by David Sims, courtesy of Balenciaga; p. 137: © Chris Moore / Catwalking / Getty Images; p. 138: Illustration: Irina Lazareanu archives / All rights reserved; © Photo12 / Alamy / Camera Press; p. 139: © Robert Fairer; p. 140–41: © Balenciaga Campaign Spring Summer 2006 - by David Sims, courtesy of Balenciaga; p. 142: Private collection; p. 145: © Emma Summerton; p. 146–47: Photo by Craig McDean / *Vogue* © The Condé Nast Publications Ltd; p. 149: Courtesy of Inez & Vinoodh; p. 151–55, 157–59: © Inez & Vinoodh; p. 152–53, 157: bkgd Irina Lazareanu and Pascal Loperena; p. 160: © François Rotger/*Marie Claire* Italy, October 2008; p. 162: Irina Lazareanu archives; p. 165: © Pennie Smith; p. 167: bkgd, tr and br Irina Lazareanu archives; all others © Malina Molgan; p. 169: bkgd and tr Irina Lazareanu archives; tl and cl © Rosalie Miller; cr © Sally Anchassi; b © Malina Molgan; p. 170: Irina Lazareanu archives; p. 171: l © Malina Molgan; r © Gavin Doyle; p. 173: Irina Lazareanu archives; p. 175: bl © Gavin Doyle; all others Irina Lazareanu archives; p. 177: tr and cr © Leo Haddad; all others Irina Lazareanu archives; p. 179: bkgd Irina Lazareanu archives; tr © Damien McFadden; bl and br © Malina Molgan; bc © Shaun Bailey / WENN / SIPA; p. 181: © Malina Molgan; p. 182: © Philip Gay; p. 183: © Leo Haddad; p. 185: © Photo12 / ABC / Y.R.; p. 187: b © Stephanie K. Nihon; all others Irina Lazareanu archives; p. 188–89: © Jan Welters; p. 191: Irina Lazareanu archives / All rights reserved; p. 192–93: bkgd Irina Lazareanu archives / Portrait © Jen Carey; all others © Sally Anchassi; p. 194: © Bryan Adams CAMERAPRESS / GAMMA-RAPHO; p. 197: © Kevin Mazur / WireImage; p. 199: bkgd and t Irina Lazareanu archives; b © Beretta / Sims / Shutterstock; p. 201: bkgd and b Irina Lazareanu archives; t © Gareth Cattermole / AFP; p. 203: © Ross Gilmore / Redferns; p. 205: © Stas Komarovski; p. 207: © Mike Marsland / WireImage; p. 209: © Stas Komarovski; p. 210–11: © JMEnternational / Redferns; p. 212: © Jen Carey; p. 215: © Jen Carey; p. 217: bkgd Irina Lazareanu archives / © François Rotger; tl © BILLY FARRELL / Patrick McMullan via Getty Images; c Irina Lazareanu archives; b © Laura Marie Cieplik; all others © Gavin Doyle; p. 219: bkgd Irina Lazareanu archives; tl © Laura Marie Cieplik; c © BP Fallon; all others © Gavin Doyle; p. 220: © Sleiman Dayaa; p. 221: Irina Lazareanu archives; p. 223: © Lawrence Lucier / FilmMagic; p. 225: © James Devaney / WireImage; p. 227: © Gavin Doyle; p. 228–29: © Jen Carey; p. 230: © Philip Gay; p. 233: © Greg Kadel; p. 235: bkgd © Sean Lennon; tr © Sasha Eisenman / *Jalouse*; all others © Greg Kadel; p. 237: bkgd Irina Lazareanu archives; all others © Jen Carey; p. 238: © Michel Dufour / WireImage; p. 239: © Jan Welters; p. 240: © Jen Carey; p. 241: © Rosalie Miller; p. 242: © Kristin Vicari; p. 243: © Robert Fairer; p. 244–45: © Greg Kadel; p. 246: © Leslie Kee; p. 249: © Allan Tannenbaum / Getty Images; p. 251: bkgd Irina Lazareanu archives; c © Irina Lazareanu; tr and b © Greg Kadel; p. 253: bkgd and cl Irina Lazareanu archives; tl Raegan Glazner; tc and tr © Roberta Findlay; cr © Wendell Teodoro / WireImage; bl © Keystone / Hulton Archive / Getty Images; br © Sasha Eisenman / *Jalouse;* p. 255: Photo by Iain Macmillan © Yoko Ono Lennon; p. 256: © Greg Kadel; p. 257: Photo by David Nutter © Yoko Ono Lennon; p. 258–59: © Koh Hasebe / Shinko Music / Getty Images; p. 261: © François Rotger

Text Credits

Editorial Director
Kate Mascaro

Curator
Pascal Loperena

Manuscript Development
Drew McConnell

Runway Bird Chief Operating Officer
Sally Anchassi

Strategic Advisor
Cheri Bowen

Photo Research
Irina Lazareanu and Marie-Catherine Audet

Collages
Irina Lazareanu and Pascal Loperena

Design and Typesetting
Claude-Olivier Four

Cover Design
Audrey Sednaoui

Editor
Helen Adedotun

Proofreading
Bethany Wright

Production
Louisa Hanifi-Morard and Titouan Roland

Color Separation
Atelier Frédéric Claudel, Paris

Printer
GPS Group, Bosnia and Herzegovina

© Flammarion, S.A., Paris, 2022

Simultaneously published in French as
*Carnets de Style Rock:
Conseils d'un Top Model*
© Flammarion, S.A., Paris, 2022

22 23 24 3 2 1

ISBN: 978-2-08-020696-1
Legal Deposit: 03/2022